RECIPE

Everyday
Quilts

Rita
Fishel

AQS Publishing

Dedication

Located in Paducah, Kentucky, the American Quilter's Society (AQS) is dedicated to promoting the accomplishments of today's quilters. Through its publications and events, AQS strives to honor today's quiltmakers and their work and to inspire future creativity and innovation in quiltmaking.

Executive Book Editor: Andi Milam Reynolds
Additional Editing: Linda Baxter Lasco
Copy Editor: Chrystal Abhalter
Graphic Design: Lynda Smith
Cover Design: Michael Buckingham
Quilt Photography: Charles R. Lynch

Additional copies of this book may be ordered from the American Quilter's Society, PO Box 3290, Paducah, KY 42002-3290, or online at www.AmericanQuilter.com.

Library of Congress Cataloging-in-Publication Data

Fishel, Rita.
  Everyday quilts / by Rita Fishel.
    p. cm.
  ISBN 978-1-57432-681-9
  1. Quilting--Patterns. I. Title.
  TT835.F5663 2011
  746.46--dc22
                          2011000918

This book is dedicated to the faithful staff and wonderful friends of Creations SewClever, my quilt shop in Chillicothe, Ohio.

Without their encouragement, their assistance, and their tireless attempts to keep me on track, this book would never have been possible. Here's to:

Jan Bost, my exceptional shop manager;
Linda Burton and Charlotte Routt, who travel the globe with me in search of new customers;
Megan Detty, Becki Smith, Becky Wilson, Vicki Rearley, Carol Hixson, Rose Poling, Pam Herron, Kay Appel, Stevie Jarvis, and Dawn Oyer, who keep the home fires burning; and
my dearest friend, Susie, who saw to it that books would happen.

I am grateful to my family for believing in me and supporting my dream, and to my friend Julia Cleary, without whom this would never have been possible.

You all mean the world to me.

> All location shots photographed at
> *Higdon Furniture of Paducah*.
> We appreciate their cooperation.

Contents

KISSES AND HUGS (TO SUSIE!)

SAWTOOTH PATCHWORK IRISH CHAIN

Contents (continued)

WAY TO GO!

STARS AT SEA

Introduction

This book was written to celebrate the fun I've had and the friends I've made in almost two decades as a quilt shop owner, teacher, and traveling merchant.

These quilts, made with friends, are a tangible reminder of what was going on as the quilt was being made; the memories stitched into the fabrics; the gentle conversations; the rollicking laughter; the food; the people; the intentions. Lucky me, this is the story of every day of my life.

To give you a jump start on making your own everyday quilts, in this book I've combined fun quilts with companion stories and tasty recipes, and thrown in a few hints and "snips"—words of wisdom.

Share the joy of creating by quilting with friends, stitching memories, and cooking up a storm! May you always be blessed with good fabric, good friends, good food, and good times!

WINDOW OVER MANHATTAN

STEPS TO THE ALTAR

Chain Chain Chain

60" x 70"

Cremations SewClever – or –
How Much Fabric Can We Store in a Casket?

It was the long-awaited moving day from our old quilt shop (I own Creations SewClever in Chillicothe, Ohio) to a new space. We'd just purchased a big, beautiful, nineteenth-century funeral home and were dying (ha!) to have more room.

A friend who worked with inmates arranged for five of them to help us move as part of their community service. While this gang schlepped merchandise, store manager Jan and I directed and organized as our employees helped move.

At lunch we had a surprise party for Jan with birthday cake, candles, and singing. Then it was back to work. At 4 p.m. Jan and I went back to the old shop to finish cleaning.

As we drove, Jan said, "Rita, you always outdo yourself when you celebrate my birthday, but this one will be hard to top." I said, "Really, it was nothing." She replied, "I've never, ever been serenaded by convicts."

Yardage & Cutting
All strips are cut their measurement by 40" (width of fabric).

Fabric	Yardage	First Cut	Second Cut
Feature	3½ yards	3 strips 6½"	15 squares 6½" x 6½"
		2 strips 8½"	30 rectangles 2½" x 8½"
		2 strips 6½"	30 rectangles 2½" x 6½"
		2 strips 2½"	30 squares 2½" x 2½"
		3 strips 3½"	30 squares 3½" x 3½"
		7 strips 4½" for outer border	
		7 strips 3" for binding	
Contrast	⅔ yard	4 strips 2½"	60 squares 2½" x 2½"
		3 strips 3½"	30 squares 3½" x 3½"
Background	1 yard	4 strips 6½"	60 rectangles 2½" x 6½"
		6 strips 1½" for inner border	
Backing	3¾ yards		
Batting	68" x 78"		
Binding	See feature		

Step 1
Make 30
Make 15

Step 2
Make 15

Step 3
Make 30
Make 15

Step 4
Make 15

Step 5
Make 15

Step 1

Sew together 30 pairs of 3½" x 3½" feature and contrast squares. Press the seam toward the contrast square.

Using those 30 pairs, sew them into 15 Four-Patch units. Press well.

Step 2

Sew 1 feature 2½" x 6½" rectangle to opposite sides of each Four-Patch unit. Press the seams toward the rectangles.

Step 3

Sew 1 contrast 2½" x 2½" square to each 2½" x 8½" feature rectangle. Press the seam toward the feature rectangle.

Sew the Step 3 units to the top and bottom of the Step 2 units, reversing the position of the contrast squares so they form a chain through the finished block. Match seams and press toward the newly added strips. The block should measure 10½" x 10½".

Step 4

Sew 1 background 2½" x 6½" rectangle to opposite sides of each 6½" x 6½" feature square. Press the seams toward the rectangles.

Step 5

Sew 1 feature 2½" x 2½" square and 1 contrast 2½" x 2½" square to opposite ends of each remaining 2½" x 6½" background rectangle. Press the seams toward the rectangles. Sew these units to the Step 4 units, matching seams. The block should measure 10½" x 10½".

Snips

Quilting alone is an out-of-buddy experience!

Step 6

Sew the blocks from Step 3 and Step 5 into 3 rows starting with a Step 3 block. Pay attention to the chain orientation.

Step 7

Use the remaining Step 3 and Step 5 blocks to sew 3 more rows starting with a Step 5 block.

Step 8

Assemble the top according to the sample quilt photo. Press.

Step 9

Add the inner border by first squaring the top. Then measure through the quilt top center vertically to determine the side border length. Piece border strips together end-to-end if necessary, trim them to the desired length, and pin one to each side. Sew. Press seams toward the border.

Repeat to add the top and bottom borders, measuring horizontally through the center of the quilt (which now includes the side borders).

Square the top again if necessary and repeat the measuring/piecing sequence to add the outer border. Press and admire!!

You're ready to layer the top with batting and backing, baste the layers, quilt as desired, and bind and label your quilt.

Optional flange: To add a contrasting flange as shown in the alternate colorway on page 11, choose a fabric that will bring out one of the less obvious colors in your fabric—a zinger. This choice should enhance your finished quilt and either brighten it or make all of the colors "pop" with the tiny zing you use. It doesn't need to be a solid fabric, but it should "read" solid. (Any fabric pattern will be lost in the tiny bit of flange that shows.)

Step 6

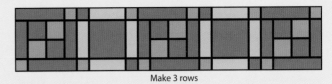

Make 3 rows

Step 7

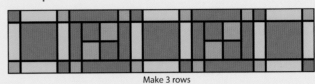

Make 3 rows

A flange will not alter the finished size of your quilt. I recommend cutting ¾" strips of this zinger. Cut as many strips as you cut for the border to which it will be sewn.

Shorten your machine stitch length somewhat and sew all of these ¾" strips together end-to-end into one long strip. Press the seams open. Press the flange in half lengthwise, right-side out.

Hint

When rotary cutting through multiple layers of fabric, if you reach across the width of fabric and make a cut through all layers at the far end of your ruler, then cut as normal, that first cut will lock the layers in place so they won't slide on each other.

CHAIN CHAIN CHAIN

Lengthen your machine stitch to a bit longer than you used to piece your top (but not as long as a basting stitch). With raw edges together and a ⅛" seam allowance, carefully sew the flange down both long sides of the quilt. Trim the ends and then sew a flange across the top and bottom of the quilt. Press the finished flange to this border— not toward the border that will be sewn next.

Now you are ready to add the next border. Sew this as you normally would (down the long sides then across the top and bottom) *except as you sew, place the border strip being added against the feed dogs with the back of the quilt top facing up.*

This allows you to see the stitching that is holding the flange in place so you are sure to keep the flange seam inside the ¼" seam allowance. *Be VERY careful to sew an ACCURATE ¼" seam allowance* as you complete this step.

The flange is deliberately tiny; any wiggle in your seam allowance will show very clearly if it's uneven. Although you must be careful, adding a zingy flange is easy and spices things up, so don't be afraid to give it a try. Hey—you have a seam ripper if you aren't happy with your results! Most likely you will look at your completed top and say, "Wow!" Add any additional borders, square the top, layer, baste, quilt, bind, and label.

Take No Prisoners Vegetable Salad

(Add or adjust veggies as desired)

1 bag frozen broccoli and cauliflower (thawed and drained)
1 can garbanzo beans or chickpeas (drained)
1 can green beans (drained)
1 can pitted black olives (drained)
2 tomatoes, chopped (or several cherry tomatoes, sliced)
½ red onion, sliced very thin

Combine all ingredients in a large bowl. Toss with ½ cup of your favorite Italian or Greek salad dressing plus ¼ cup French dressing. Chill or serve at room temperature. Top with crumbled feta cheese if desired.

Make just 6 each of step 3 and step 5 blocks, change the placement, add cornerstones to the inner border and a flange, and use a different binding fabric. Voilá! A 40" x 50" alternate colorway and size of CHAIN CHAIN CHAIN.

Window Over Manhattan

60" x 70"

Everyday Quilts ❖ Rita Fishel

If You Can Make It There – or – Big Blisters in the Big Apple

After a long day of walking endless miles in and around Manhattan, the five tired Fishel girls enjoyed a matinee performance of *Mama Mia!* on Broadway. We were two rows from the back on the aisle. Next to me *in* the aisle was an usher who was a dead ringer for the Niles Crane character from the television show *Frasier*.

As the upbeat performance came to an end, after the ovations and curtain calls, the cast broke into another 30 minutes of singing and dancing to lively Abba tunes. The entire audience was on its feet, clapping, singing along, and dancing.

Next to me in the aisle "Niles" seemed part of the cast. He performed the complete revue singing,

dancing, and making the same hand gestures and facial expressions as the male chorus dancers. He was in his glory! And in his own world. I'd bet he was in the original musical years ago. I had to have one eye on him and one on the stage as I sang and clapped and danced with the rest of the audience. What a treat!

Months later our New York daughter, Shannon, met several friends after work for drinks and fun. One brought a friend, Jim, the stage manager for *Mama Mia!* Jim brought a friend to the gathering, too—none other than our very own Niles! It's a small world—even in NYC!

Yardage & Cutting

All strips are cut their measurement by 40" (width of fabric).

Fabric	Yardage	First Cut	Second Cut
Feature	3⅛ yards	7 strips 6½"	50 rectangles 4½" x 6½"
		7 strips 5½" for outer border	
		7 strips 3" for binding	
Contrast	⅓ yard	6 strips 1½" for middle border	
Coordinate	1 yard	7 strips 4½"	50 squares 4½" x 4½"
Background	1 yard	1 strip 8½"	20 rectangles 8½" x 1½"
		6 strips 1½"	
		6 strips 2½" for inner border	
Backing	3¾ yards		
Batting	68" x 78"		
Binding	See feature		

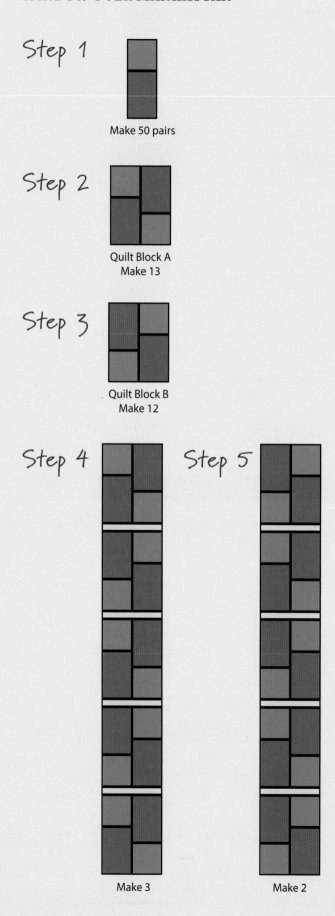

Step 1

Make 50 pairs

Step 2

Quilt Block A
Make 13

Step 3

Quilt Block B
Make 12

Step 4

Step 5

Make 3   Make 2

Step 1

Sew 1 coordinate 4½" x 4½" square to each feature 4½" x 6½" rectangle. Press the seam toward the coordinate square.

Step 2

Sew 26 Step 1 units together to make 13 A blocks. Press seams well.

Step 3

Using the remaining 24 pairs from Step 1, sew them to each other to form 12 B blocks. These will be mirror images of Block A. Press seams well.

Step 4

Sew 3 A blocks and 2 B blocks together, joining them with 8½" x 1½" background sashing strips. Press the seams toward the sashing. Make 3 columns, which should measure 54½". Set columns aside.

Step 5

Sew 3 B blocks and 2 A blocks together, joining them with 8½" x 1½" background sashing strips. Press the seams toward the sashing. Make 2 columns, which should measure 54½". Set columns aside.

Step 6

Sew the 6 background 1½" strips together, end-to-end, into one long strip. Press the seams open. Cut them into 4 lengths the measurement of your completed columns.

Step 7

Using the quilt photo (page 16) as a guide, sew the completed columns together beginning and ending with a column from Step 4.

Use pins to hold the sashing strips in place as you sew. For best results, match the ends of the rows with the ends of the background strips AND match the vertical background sashing strips with those in preceding columns. Press all the seams toward the horizontal sashing strips.

Step 8

Add background, contrast, and feature fabric borders, respectively.

Add the inner (background) border by first squaring the top. Then measure through the quilt top center vertically to determine the side border length. Piece border strips together end-to-end if necessary, trim them to the desired length, and pin one to each side.

For a perfect border fit, quarter the top and borders to create pin placement marks: fold each in half, crease, then in half again and crease. Use the crease marks as you pin raw edges together, starting at the center. If needed, ease in fullness within quarters. Repeat to add the top and bottom borders, measuring horizontally through the center of the quilt (which now includes the side borders).

Square the top again if necessary and repeat the measuring/piecing sequence to add the contrast (middle) and feature (outer) borders. Press and admire!!

You're ready to square the top, layer it with batting and backing, baste the layers, quilt as desired, and bind and label your quilt.

Step 8

Alternate colorway with wider middle border. 62½" x 71½".

Manhattan Sausage Bars

1 lb bulk sausage

½ bag of frozen onions and peppers

2 tubes of refrigerated crescent roll dough

8 oz cream cheese, softened

shredded cheddar cheese to taste

Sauté sausage, onions, and peppers until cooked through, breaking it into fine crumbles as you cook. Drain. Turn the heat to low, add cream cheese. Stir until blended through the mixture.

On a greased cookie sheet spread one tube of crescent roll dough as if making a pizza crust. Patch all tears and holes. Spread sausage mixture across the dough. Top with the remaining tube of dough, spreading to cover. Pinch the edges to keep the filling contained.

Sprinkle shredded cheddar on top and bake at 350 degrees for 20–30 minutes, or until top is bubbly and golden. Cool slightly and cut into bars.

Snips

"When your work speaks for itself, don't interrupt."

Henry J. Kaiser

Feel the Love

58" x 70"

Rollin' on the River – or –
Could We Really Be Arrested for This?

After a long day working the AQS quilt show in Nashville, nine of us planned to take a paddle-wheel cruise on the Cumberland River. Our tickets didn't include dinner, but we were assured we could bring our own food and enjoy a picnic on the deck. We packed a cooler.

Before embarking on the ship, a friend surprised me with a 5-liter box of wine. As we approached the ship, I noticed a sign: "Positively NO food or alcohol will be permitted on board. Purses and packages subject to search."

Hating to waste food (and wine), we asked for ticket refunds. The ship's captain offered to comp us dinner, and another cruiser volunteered to put our cooler in her truck. Bumped from "steerage" to "first class," we enjoyed a lovely dinner and a Vegas-style show.

The next day I ran into another cruiser who said, "I met someone who told me about this bunch of folks who were trying to take food and alcohol onto the ship. Can you imagine!?" This quilt was made in honor of the folks of the friendly South.

Yardage & Cutting

All strips are cut their measurement by 40" (width of fabric).

Fabric	Yardage	First Cut	Second Cut
Feature	2⅔ yards	10 strips 3½"	104 squares 3½" x 3½"
		7 strips 4½" (outer border)	
		7 strips 3" (binding)	
Contrast	⅔ yard	5 strips 3½"	55 squares 3½" x 3½" + 1 square from the remains of the 4" strip (below)
		1 strip 4"	8 squares 4" x 4"
Background	1⅔ yards	6 strips 3½"	64 squares 3½" x 3½"
		4 strips 6½"	40 rectangles 3½" x 6½"
		1 strip 4"	8 squares 4" x 4"
		1 strip 2½"	16 squares 2½" x 2½"
		1 strip 2"	16 squares 2" x 2"
Inner border	⅓ yard	6 strips 1½"	
Backing	3⅔ yards		
Batting	66" x 78"		
Binding	See feature		

Step 1

Make 64

Step 1

Sew together 64 pairs of 3½" x 3½" feature and background squares. Press the seam toward the feature square.

Step 2

Make 40

Step 2

Sew 1 background 3½" x 6½" rectangle to each of 40 Step 1 pairs. Press the seam toward the rectangle.

Step 3

Make 12

Step 3

Sew the remaining 24 Step 1 pairs into 12 Four-Patch units. Press well.

Step 4

Make 40

Step 4

Sew 40 contrast 3½" x 3½" squares and 40 feature 3½" x 3½" squares together. Press the seam toward the feature square.

Step 5

Make 20

Step 5

Sew the Step 4 pairs into 20 Four-Patch units. Press well. From this point on the quilt will lay flatter if the seams are pressed open.

Step 6

Make 16

Step 6

Place 8 contrast 4" x 4" squares against 8 background 4" x 4" squares, right sides together. Using a pencil or chalk marker, draw a diagonal line across each pair from corner to corner. Sew ¼" on each side of the drawn line. Cut on the drawn line. Press the seam open. Square each of the resulting 16 half-square triangles to 3½" x 3½".

Step 7

Place 1 background 2½" x 2½" square against the top right-hand corner of 1 contrast 3½" x 3½" square, right sides together. Draw a line from corner to corner on the smaller square. Sew on that line. Make 16.

Trim ¼" from the stitching and press the triangle up to make a square.

Divide these 16 squares into 2 piles of 8 each, arranged in mirror image like this:

On the upper outside corner of each unit place a 2" x 2" background square. Repeat the drawing-stitching-trimming-pressing process to make 8 units of each.

Step 8

Sew the Step 6 units together. Press the seam open.

Step 9

Sew the Step 7 units together. Press the seam open.

Step 10

Sew the Step 8 units to the Step 9 units to make Heart blocks. Press the seams toward the top of the Heart block.

Step 7

Make 16

Press

Arrange in mirror-image piles

Make 8 of each

Step 8

Make 8

Step 9

Make 8

Step 10

Make 8

Step 11

Make 12

Step 11

Sew together 1 Step 2 unit with 1 Step 3 Four-Patch. Then sew together 1 Step 5 Four-Patch and 1 Step 2 unit. Join these to make a unit. Press the seams open.

Step 12

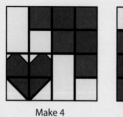

Make 4   Make 4

Step 12

Sew together 1 Step 2 unit with 1 Step 5 Four-Patch. Then sew together 1 Step 10 Heart block with 1 Step 2 unit. Join these to make a block. Notice the Heart block orientations (4 each). Press the seams open.

Step 13

Assemble the quilt top:

Step 13

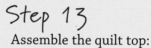

Row 1

Row 2

Row 3

Row 4

Row 5

Step 14

For a perfect border fit, quarter the top and borders to create pin placement marks: fold each in half, crease, then in half again and crease. Use the crease marks as you pin raw edges together, starting at the center. If needed, ease in fullness within quarters.

Add the inner border by first squaring the top. Then measure through the quilt top center vertically to determine the side border length. Piece border strips together end-to-end if necessary, trim them to the desired length, and pin one to each side.

Repeat to add the top and bottom borders, measuring horizontally through the center of the quilt (which now includes the side borders).

Square the top again if necessary and repeat the measuring/piecing sequence to add the outer border. Press and admire!!

You're ready to layer the top with batting and backing, baste the layers, quilt as desired, and bind and label your quilt.

Hint

Do you save all your old sewing machine needles? Try using them to hang pictures. Pound them into the wall up to the thick part of the needle. They work great! Reduce-Reuse-Recycle.

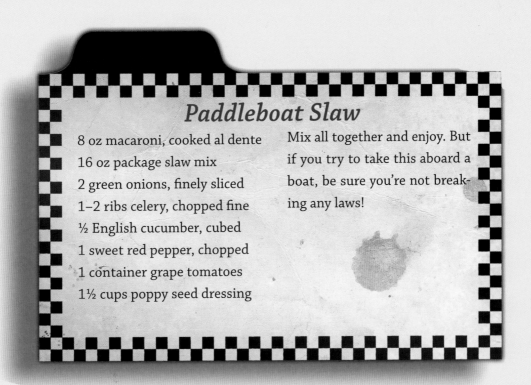

Paddleboat Slaw

8 oz macaroni, cooked al dente
16 oz package slaw mix
2 green onions, finely sliced
1–2 ribs celery, chopped fine
½ English cucumber, cubed
1 sweet red pepper, chopped
1 container grape tomatoes
1½ cups poppy seed dressing

Mix all together and enjoy. But if you try to take this aboard a boat, be sure you're not breaking any laws!

Kisses and Hugs (to Susie!)

71½" x 81"

A Moveable Feast – or – The Third Time's the Charm!

One week before my Quilt Away, I called the hotel to confirm rooms. To my horror, they did NOT have my reservation date correct and were booked completely full! I had quilters coming and no place for them to play! In desperation I booked a hotel 20 miles north of our shop. It was old, not clean, poorly lit, and I couldn't bear to think about what else might be wrong. But it was big. I told the manager I was coming back with a scrub bucket and light bulbs. Then I contacted all 50 registered quilters coming from various states and told them we were moving to Plan B.

No sooner had I called everyone, feeling quite foolish, when my dear friend Susie phoned. Three days before our event, my angel-friend had taken it upon herself to go to the nicest hotel in our little town and see about the possibility of having our Quilt Away there. Catering restrictions had discouraged me from contacting them. They had rooms and a banquet hall available! Having just completed a $2 million renovation, it was sparkling clean with lots of space, windows, and electric outlets. They were more interested in booking their facility than making their caterer happy, so we signed a contract and we were IN—50 quilters and *my* caterer. Now to tell everyone about Plan C.

Yardage & Cutting

All strips are cut their measurement by 40" (width of fabric).

Fabric	Yardage	First Cut	Second Cut
Feature	3 yards	3 strips 10"	11 squares 10" x 10"; cut diagonally twice to make 44 triangles (You'll have extra.)
		8 strips 5½" for outer border	
		8 strips 3" for binding	
Contrast	1¾ yards (sashing bars & center diamonds)*	2 strips 3¼"	21* squares 3¼" x 3¼" (if you want these to be a separate color you need ⅓ yard)
		5 strips 8½"	97 rectangles 2" x 8½"
Coordinate A	1 yard	3 strips 10"	11 squares 10" x 10"; cut diagonally twice to make 44 triangles (You'll have extra.)
Coordinate B	1¼ yards	6 strips 4½"	84 rectangles 2½" x 4½"
		7 strips 2" for inner border	
Background	1 yard	3 strips 2"	60 squares 2" x 2"
		6 strips 2½"	84 squares 2½" x 2½"
		3 strips 4½"	21 squares 4½" x 4½"; cut diagonally twice to make 84 triangles
Backing	5½ yards		
Batting	80" x 89"		
Binding	See feature		

Step 1

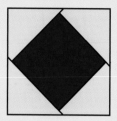

Make 21

Step 2

Make 21

Step 3

Make 42

Step 4

Make 21

Step 5

Make 21

Step 6

Make 12   Make 9

Step 1

Use: 21 contrast 3¼" x 3¼" squares

84 background triangles

Sew 2 background triangles to opposite sides of 1 contrast square. Press the seams toward the triangles. Repeat on the remaining 2 sides. Square up and trim excess background leaving a 4½" square with ¼" seam allowance at the 4 points of the diamond as shown.

Step 2

Use: 42 coordinate B 2½" x 4½" rectangles

Sew 2 of these onto opposite sides of the blocks completed in Step 1. Press the seams toward the rectangles.

Step 3

Use: 42 coordinate B 2½" x 4½" rectangles

84 background 2½" x 2½" squares

Sew 1 background square to both ends of the 42 coordinate B rectangles. Press the seams toward the rectangles.

Step 4

Sew the 42 units completed in Step 3 to the unfinished sides of the 21 blocks from Step 2. Press the seams toward the rectangles.

Step 5

Use: 42 feature triangles

42 coordinate A triangles

Sew these pieces together in diagonal Four-Patch blocks. Press the seams toward the coordinate A triangles. Square this block to 8½" x 8½".

Step 6

Use: 21 Step 5 blocks

42 contrast 2" x 8½" rectangles

Sew 2 contrast rectangles to opposite sides of 1 diagonal Four-Patch from Step 5. Press seams toward the contrast bars.

Step 7

Use: 48 contrast 2" x 8½" rectangles (You will have 49 left; set them aside.)

56 background 2" x 2" squares

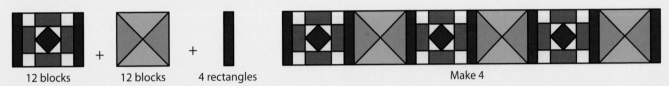

Make 8

Sew these into 8 rows, beginning and ending each row with a background square. Press the seams toward the rectangles.

Step 8

Assemble Step 8 rows. Sew these into 4 rows. Press the seams toward the rectangles.

12 blocks   +   12 blocks   +   4 rectangles

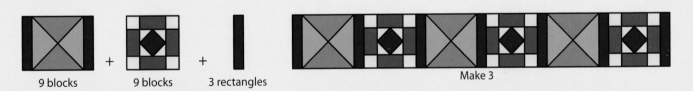

Make 4

Step 9

Assemble Step 9 rows. Sew these into 3 rows. Press the seams toward the rectangles.

9 blocks   +   9 blocks   +   3 rectangles

Make 3

Hint

Buy a little extra fabric when shopping for quilt yardage and plan to make matching pillowcases. With ¾ yard of fabric for the pillowcase, and ¼ yard of a coordinate for the cuff, you'll accessorize that beautiful quilt in a jiffy!

Fold the ¾ yard piece right sides together 27" x 22" and sew across one end and up the side, leaving the top open.

Fold the cuff right sides together 9" x 22" and sew just the 9" side. Fold the sewn cuff in half, right sides out, as it would look on the pillowcase. Pin the cuff to the pillowcase, with the cuff tucked inside the pillowcase, right sides together and raw edges together. Match seams together. Stitch. Zigzag or serge the raw edges to finish them. Turn the pillowcase right-side out, press it well, and topstitch the cuff seam allowance away from the cuff.

Step 10

Use the 8 Step 7 rows plus Steps 8 and 9 rows to follow the assembly diagram, and sew all rows together. Press all seams toward the rectangles in the Step 7 rows.

Borders

For the inner border, sew the coordinate B 2" strips end-to-end. Press the seams open.

Add the inner border by first squaring the top. Then measure through the quilt top center vertically and horizontally. Write these measurements down and cut 2 border strips for each measurement. Piece border strips together end-to-end if necessary and trim them to the desired length.

For a perfect border fit, quarter the top and borders to create pin placement marks: fold each in half, crease, then in half again and crease. Use the crease marks as you pin raw edges together, starting at the center. If needed, ease in fullness within quarters. Sew the long inner borders to the sides of the quilt. Press the seams toward the border.

Sew 1 background 2" x 2" square to each end of the remaining 2 inner border strips. Press the seams away from the cornerstones. Quarter the top and bottom of the quilt and do the same to the borders. Pin and sew. Note: You will need to match the cornerstones to the lengthwise borders already sewn to your quilt. Press the seams toward the border.

For the outer border, sew the feature 5½" strips end-to-end. Press the seams open. Sew this border down both long sides of your quilt. Press seams to this new border and square-up the 4 corners of your quilt so as not to distort the growing quilt. Repeat this across the top and the bottom of your quilt. Press and square the corners. Admire your beautiful quilt!!

You're ready to square the top, layer it with batting and backing, baste the layers, quilt as desired, and bind and label your quilt.

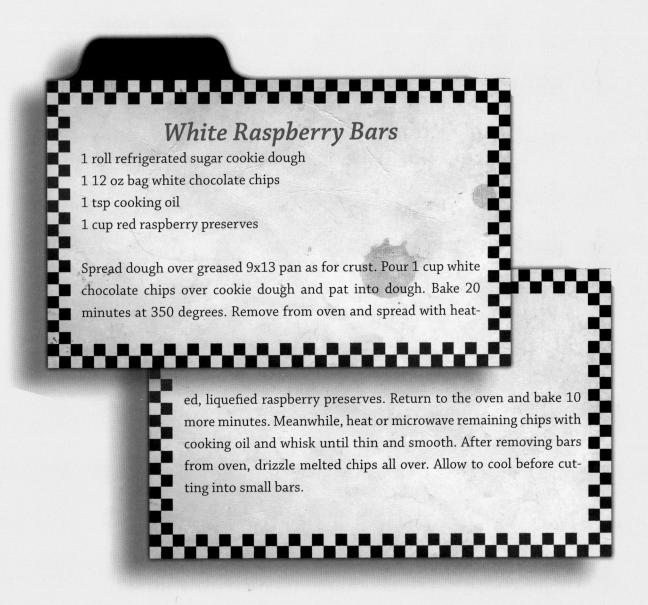

White Raspberry Bars

1 roll refrigerated sugar cookie dough
1 12 oz bag white chocolate chips
1 tsp cooking oil
1 cup red raspberry preserves

Spread dough over greased 9x13 pan as for crust. Pour 1 cup white chocolate chips over cookie dough and pat into dough. Bake 20 minutes at 350 degrees. Remove from oven and spread with heat-

ed, liquefied raspberry preserves. Return to the oven and bake 10 more minutes. Meanwhile, heat or microwave remaining chips with cooking oil and whisk until thin and smooth. After removing bars from oven, drizzle melted chips all over. Allow to cool before cutting into small bars.

A Path Less Traveled

96" x 108"

Just Call Me Grace – or –
A Black Boot Really Does Go with Every Occasion

Heading out of the shop at a run, I stumbled right out of my flip-flops and onto my rear. I was unable to walk, so my staff carted me to the emergency room. They diagnosed three broken foot bones.

Snugly cast in a black boot, I realized I'd need to be on crutches during International Quilt Market the next week. I hated to think about navigating the airports, but to my surprise and delight I was driven around on one of those cool electric trams.

When I landed in Houston a wheelchair attendant met me. My traveling companions said, "Wow! It was so nice of the airline to call ahead to help you!" The youngster pushing me said, "Oh, we always have a wheelchair here for the seniors."

Yardage & Cutting

All strips are cut their measurement by 40" (width of fabric).

Fabric	Yardage	First Cut	Second Cut
Feature	5¼ yards	7 strips 6½"	42 squares 6½" x 6½"
		6 strips 4½"	42 squares 4½" x 4½"
		10 strips 7½" for outer border	
		10 strips 3" for binding	
Contrast fabric	2½ yards	8 strips 3½"	84 squares 3½" x 3½"
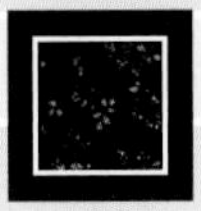		6 strips 4½"	42 squares 4½" x 4½"
		8 strips 3½" for inner border	
Coordinate	2¾ yards	6 strips 4½"	84 rectangles 2½" x 4½"
		6 strips 6½"	84 rectangles 2½" x 6½"
		9 strips 2½" for second border	
Background	1¼ yards	8 strips 3½"	cut 88 squares 3½" x 3½"
		1 strip 2½"	4 squares 2½" x 2½"
		9 strips ¾" for flange	
Backing	9 yards		
Batting	105" x 117"		
Binding	See feature		

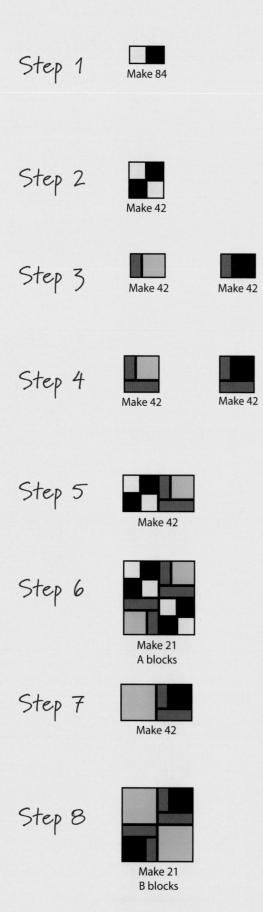

Step 1
Make 84

Step 2
Make 42

Step 3
Make 42   Make 42

Step 4
Make 42   Make 42

Step 5
Make 42

Step 6
Make 21
A blocks

Step 7
Make 42

Step 8
Make 21
B blocks

Step 1

Sew together 84 pairs of 3½" x 3½" background and contrast squares. Press the seam toward the dark square. You will have 4 squares of background left. Set them aside for inner border cornerstones (Step 11).

Step 2

Sew these pairs into 42 Four-Patch units. Press the seams open.

Step 3

Sew 1 coordinate 2½" x 4½" rectangle to each 4½"x 4½" feature square and to each contrast square. Press the seam toward the coordinate rectangle.

Step 4

Sew 1 coordinate 2½" x 6½" rectangle to each Step 3 unit. Press the seam toward the rectangle.

Step 5

Sew a Step 2 Four-Patch unit to a Step 4 feature+coordinate unit. Be sure to put the feature square in the upper right corner. Press the seam toward the coordinate rectangle.

Step 6

Sew the Step 5 units together in pairs to make 21 A blocks. Press the seams in one direction.

Step 7

Sew the 42 feature 6½" x 6½" squares and the 42 Step 4 contrast+coordinate units together. Press the seam toward the feature square.

Step 8

Sew the Step 7 units together in pairs to make 21 B blocks. Press the seams in one direction.

Step 9

Sew the A and B blocks into rows. Alternate the starting blocks. Press the seams toward the B blocks. Sew 2 rows together to make a row pair. Create 7 row pairs.

Step 9

Step 10

Sew the 7 row pairs together to create a quilt top, following the photograph on page 30. Press well.

Step 10

Step 11

This quilt has 3 borders—inner, second, and outer, with a flange between the second and outer borders.

Add the inner border by first squaring the top. Then measure through the quilt top center vertically and horizontally. Write these measurements down and

Hint

A good iron is one of your most important sewing tools!

cut 2 border strips for each measurement. Piece border strips together end-to-end if necessary and trim them to the desired length.

Sew the long inner borders to the sides of the quilt. Press the seams toward the border.

Sew 1 background 3½" x 3½" square to each end of the remaining 2 inner border strips. Press the seams away from the cornerstones. Quarter the top and bottom of the quilt and do the same to the borders. Pin and sew. Note: You will need to match the cornerstones to the lengthwise borders already sewn to your quilt. Press the seams toward the border.

Repeat this sequence for the second border and cornerstones.

To add the flange, cut as many ¾" strips as you cut for the second border.

Shorten your machine stitch length somewhat and sew all of these ¾" strips together end-to-end into 1 long strip. Press the seams open. Press the flange in half lengthwise, right-side out.

Lengthen your machine stitch to a bit longer than you used to piece your top (but not as long as a basting stitch). With raw edges together and a ⅛" seam allowance, *carefully* sew the flange down both long sides of

This alternate colorway uses fewer blocks and measures 38" x 50".

the quilt. Trim the ends and then sew a flange across the top and bottom of the quilt. Press the finished flange flat to this border— not toward the border that will be sewn next.

Now you are ready to add the outer border. Readjust your stitch length and sew this as you normally would (measuring, cutting correct lengths, quartering, and stitching down the long sides then across the top and bottom) *except as you sew, place the border strip being added against the feed dogs with the back of the quilt top facing up.*

This allows you to see the stitching that is holding the flange in place so you are sure to keep the seam inside the ¼" seam allowance. *Be VERY careful to sew an ACCURATE ¼" seam allowance as you complete this step.*

The flange is deliberately tiny; any wiggle in your seam allowance will show very clearly if it's uneven. Although you must be careful, adding a zingy flange is easy and spices things up, so don't be afraid to give it a try. Hey—you have a seam ripper if you aren't happy with your results! Most likely you will look at your completed top and say, "Wow!"

You're ready to square the top, layer it with batting and backing, baste the layers, quilt as desired, and bind and label your quilt.

Fallin' Down Good Vermicelli & Sausage

- Olive oil, divided use
- 1 lb sweet Italian sausage
- 1 lb uncooked vermicelli
  (or pasta of your choice)
- 1 bell pepper chopped (red, yellow or green, or frozen combo w/ onions)
- 1 large onion, chopped
- 4 T prepared pesto
- 4 cups grape or
  cherry tomatoes, halved
- Grated/shredded Parmesan cheese
- Fresh basil, optional

Heat 3 tablespoons of olive oil drizzled over 1 or 2 inches of water in a frying pan. Prick the sausage in several places and place it in the pan, turning occasionally. Cook the sausage until the water boils away and the meat crisps. Drain the sausage on paper towels until slightly cool, then slice into bite-size pieces.

Sauté the onion and pepper in 1 or 2 tablespoons of olive oil over medium high heat until they just begin to brown. Stir in the pesto and heat through. Meanwhile, cook the pasta in boiling salted water until al dente. Drain. Toss all ingredients together gently. Garnish with Parmesan and/or scissor-cut basil.

I do love to eat! Just about anything, actually, but I especially enjoy lighter fare like this fast, light, complete meal (even though I'm not a big sausage eater).

Steps to the Altar

78" x 90"

Message in the Meatball – or –
The Proposal

Our shop staff loves to have fun together. Some of our most fun times are at our Sleepover Sewing Parties. Many are at Susie's house where her husband, John, enjoys cooking for us. At one gathering we decided we'd give John a hand with the food; each of us brought a dish to share.

As we giggled and stitched in the sewing room, John set up our buffet. He took his plate of food into the den and we gals sat at the big dining room table. We were well into our delicious meal, chatting like magpies, when John walked into the dining room, meatball in one hand, diamond ring in the other, puzzled look on his face.

He stood in the doorway; we stopped talking. Vicki looked at her left hand. Her diamond ring was missing; she had brought the meatballs. She looked at John. He looked at her. And then he dropped to one knee and said, "Vicki, will you marry me?"

Yardage & Cutting
All strips are cut their measurement by 40" (width of fabric).

Fabric	Yardage	First Cut	Second Cut
Feature	5 yards	5 strips 9½"	30 rectangles 6½" x 9½"
		3 strips 6½"	30 rectangles 3½" x 6½"
		3 strips 3½"	30 squares 3½" x 3½"
		9 strips 6½" for outer border	
		9 strips 3" for binding	
Contrast	2¼ yards	6 strips 3½"	60 squares 3½" x 3½"
		2 strips 12½"	15 rectangles 12½" x 3½"
		8 strips 3½" for inner border	
Background	1 yard	3 strips 3½"	34 squares 3½" x 3½"; cut the last square from rectangle scraps; save 4 for the inner border
		5 strips 3½"	15 rectangles 12½" x 3½"
Backing	7½ yards		
Batting	86" x 98"		
Binding	see feature		

Step 1

Make 30

Step 2

Make 30

Step 3

Make 30

Step 4

 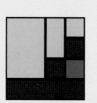

Make 15 A   Make 15 B

Step 5

Step 1

Sew together:

   30 background 3½" x 3½" squares

   30 contrast 3½" x 3½" squares

   30 feature 3½" x 3½" squares

Sew them into units with the contrast square in the center. Press the seams toward the contrast square.

Step 2

Sew together in pairs:

   30 contrast 3½" x 3½" squares

   30 feature rectangles 3½" x 6½"

Press the seam toward the contrast square.

Step 3

Using the Steps 1 and 2 units and the 30 feature 6½" x 9½" rectangles make 30 units. Press the seams toward the feature rectangle.

Step 4

Separate the Step 3 units into 2 piles of 15 each. Sew 1 contrast 12½" x 3½" rectangle across the top of 15 blocks. Sew 1 background 12½" x 3½" rectangle across the top of the other 15 blocks. Press the seam toward the rectangle.

Step 5

Using 9 Step 4 A blocks, and 6 Step 4 B blocks, make 3 rows as shown. Try to match the seams of the background and contrast squares where they meet as Four-Patch blocks. Press the seams toward the first block in the row.

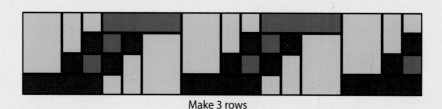

Make 3 rows

Step 6

With the 6 remaining A blocks and 9 remaining B blocks from Step 4, make 3 rows as shown. Again, try to match the seams of the background and contrast squares as you sew these blocks together. Press the seams away from the first block in the rows

Step 6

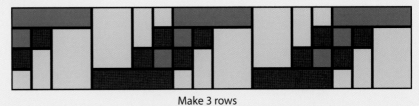

Make 3 rows

Step 7

Assemble the quilt top following the photo starting with a row from Step 5, alternating rows.

Step 7

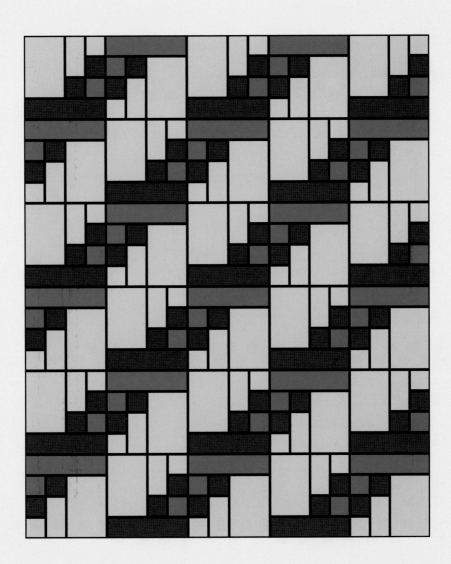

Step 8

Add the inner border by first squaring the top.

Carefully measure across the center seams of the quilt, horizontally and vertically. This is the border strip length. Piece the border strips together end-to-end if necessary and trim them to the desired length. Remeasure after each border addition to cut subsequent border strips.

For a perfect border fit, quarter the top and borders to create pin placement marks: fold each in half, crease, then in half again and crease. Use the crease marks as you pin raw edges together, starting at the center. If needed, ease in fullness within quarters.

Sew the long inner borders to the sides of the quilt. Press the seams toward the border.

Sew 1 background 3½" x 3½" square to each end of the remaining 2 inner border strips. Press the seam away from the cornerstones. Quarter the top and bottom of the quilt and do the same to the borders. Pin and sew, matching the cornerstones to the lengthwise borders already sewn to the quilt. Press the seam toward the border.

Attach the outer border, sides first. You're ready to square the top, layer it with batting and backing, baste the layers, quilt as desired, and bind and label your quilt.

My Mom's Meatballs with a Twist

2 lbs ground beef	4 T Worcestershire sauce
1 cup bread crumbs	½ cup grated Parmesan cheese
½ cup evaporated milk	1 pkg onion soup mix
2 eggs	2 T dill weed

Mix together well with hands (hint: remove rings first!) and roll into large walnut-size balls. Place on a jelly roll pan coated with cooking spray, keeping them separate. Bake at 375 degrees for 20–30 minutes, turning occasionally. Drain on paper towels.

Meatball Sauce:

2 cups tomato juice	2 onions, sliced
2 tsp sugar	4 T flour

Cook until thick. Add meatballs. Serve with hot noodles or mashed potatoes.

Snips

People are very open-minded about new things—as long
as they're exactly like the old ones.

Charles F. Kettering

Gridlock!

58" x 70"

Wearing My Adventure Hat – or –
The Show Must Go On, However Damply

It wasn't a good day for driving, but I was scheduled to give a lecture at a small rural library so I set off on the 100-mile trip through sheeting rain, cracks of thunder, and streaks of lightning. I could only sense road conditions by watching the tail lights of the truck ahead.

Well into my trip, water was cresting over small bridges and running across the road. Then the road washed out ahead. I couldn't turn around, and behind me the water continued to rise. Although I was stuck between two large semi-trucks and had no cell service, eventually sheriffs maneuvered us up and around a steep one-lane, curvy hillside.

Complete gridlock occurred when one of the trucks jackknifed on a hairpin turn, trapping me between them. After a while, local folks were able to guide me around the jackknifed truck and onto another road.

When I had cell service again I called the library, where, even though I was now nearly 2 hours late, a roomful of patient souls waited for me. The librarian directed me to her location directly across from the water tower. "No problem!" I said, "I have the tower in my sights." Imagine my surprise to learn that little village had *two* water towers!

Yardage & Cutting

All strips are cut their measurement by 40" (width of fabric).

Fabric	Yardage	First Cut	Second Cut
Feature	2⅔ yards	5 strips 2½"	80 squares 2½" x 2½"
		5 strips 4½"	80 rectangles 4½" x 2½"
		7 strips 4½" for border	
		7 strips 3" for binding	
Contrast	⅔ yard	7 strips 2½"	110 squares 2½" x 2½"
Coordinate	1 yard	3 strips 10½"	49 rectangles 2½" x 10½"
		1 strip 2½"	1 rectangle 2½" x 10½"
Background	1 yard	3 strips 4½"	40 rectangles 4½" x 2½"
		1 strip 10½"	16 rectangles 2½" x 10½"
		2 strips 2½"	4 rectangles 2½"x 10½"
Backing	3⅔ yards		
Batting	66" x 78"		
Binding	See feature		

Step 1

Make 80

Step 2

Make 80

Step 3

Make 40

Step 4

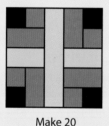

Make 20

Step 5

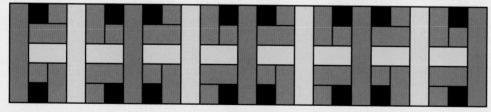

Make 5

Step 6

Make 6

Step 1

Sew together 80 pairs of 2½" x 2½" feature and contrast squares. Press the seam toward the contrast square.

Step 2

Sew the 80 feature 2½" x 4½" rectangles to the Step 1 units noting block orientation. Press the seam toward the rectangle.

Step 3

Using the Step 2 units and the 40 background 2½" x 4½" rectangles, make 40 Step 3 units. Note the direction of the blocks and make them all as shown. Press the seams toward the background rectangles.

Step 4

Use 1 background 2½" x 10½" rectangle to join a pair of Step 3 units, making sure the orientation is correct. Press the seams toward the joining rectangle.

Step 5

Count out 25 of the 2½" x 10½" coordinate rectangles. Using the Step 4 blocks, make 5 rows. Press the seams toward the coordinate rectangles.

Step 6

Using the remaining 24 coordinate 2½" x 10½" rectangles and the remaining 30 contrast 2½" x 2½" squares, make 6 rows. Press the seams toward the rectangles.

Step 7

Referring to the assembly diagram, sew the quilt top together in alternating rows, beginning and ending with Step 6 rows. Press carefully.

Step 8

You can add a flange or just add a border. Either way, square the top.

To add a flange, you will need additional fabric, and that fabric could be a zinger from your stash. Cut as many ¾" strips as you cut for the border.

Shorten your machine stitch length somewhat and sew all of these ¾" strips together end-to-end into 1 long strip. Press the seams open. Press the flange in half lengthwise, right-side out.

Lengthen your machine stitch to a bit longer than you used to piece your top (but not as long as a basting stitch). With raw edges together and a ⅛" seam allowance, *carefully* sew the flange down both long sides of the quilt. Trim the ends and then sew a flange across the top and bottom of the quilt. Press the finished flange to the top—not toward the border that will be sewn next.

Now you are ready to add the border. Sew this as you normally would (down the long sides then across the top and bottom) *except as you sew, place the border strip being added against the feed dogs with the back of the quilt top facing up.*

This allows you to see the stitching that is holding the flange in place so you are sure to keep the seam inside the ¼" seam allowance. *Be VERY careful to sew an AC-CURATE ¼" seam allowance as you complete this step.*

The flange is deliberately tiny; any wiggle in your seam allowance will show very clearly if it's uneven. Although you must be careful, adding a zingy flange is easy and spices things up, so don't be afraid to give it a try.

Hey—you have a seam ripper if you aren't happy with your results!

To add the border, measure through the quilt top center vertically to determine the side border length. Piece border strips together end-to-end if necessary, trim them to the desired length, and pin one to each side.

Repeat to add the top and bottom borders, measuring horizontally through the center of the quilt (which now includes the side borders).

You're ready to square the top, layer it with batting and backing, baste the layers, quilt as desired, and bind and label your quilt.

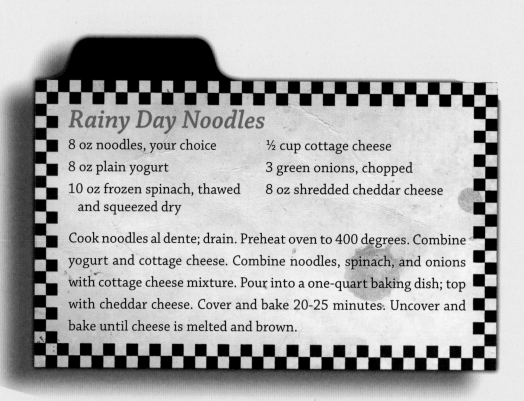

Rainy Day Noodles

8 oz noodles, your choice

8 oz plain yogurt

10 oz frozen spinach, thawed and squeezed dry

½ cup cottage cheese

3 green onions, chopped

8 oz shredded cheddar cheese

Cook noodles al dente; drain. Preheat oven to 400 degrees. Combine yogurt and cottage cheese. Combine noodles, spinach, and onions with cottage cheese mixture. Pour into a one-quart baking dish; top with cheddar cheese. Cover and bake 20-25 minutes. Uncover and bake until cheese is melted and brown.

Hint

When you cut your quilt projects before you are actually ready to sew them, it's a good idea to put little sticky labels on your pieces so you can identify them correctly when you are ready to quilt.

Way to Go!

76" x 91"

Does Sewjourner Really Quilt? – or –
Only the Ghostly Know, Mostly

Soon after moving into our new shop, we began to notice a resident who was neither paying rent nor ringing sales on our register. Interestingly, we were not the only ones to notice this presence. Over the years several customers have mentioned seeing him in an overcoat and a fedora. Aside from making noises, pushing things off mantles, or opening doors, he's pretty well-behaved and we coexist for the most part, in peace.

However, one Sunday afternoon Charlotte was in the shop by herself, machine quilting on Sewfee, one of our three longarm machines. She was startled by a scraping and banging noise in the room where she was quilting. A bit unnerved, she focused on her quilting and ignored the distraction. The noise reoccurred. When Charlotte ignored the disturbance yet again, the scissors suddenly slid across her machine table and hit the floor!

That did it! Charlotte grabbed the scissors, snatched her purse, and ran down the stairs and out the door. The next morning she brought the scissors back and confessed her hurried exit leaving the radio on and lights blazing.

Yardage & Cutting

All strips are cut their measurement by 40" (width of fabric). Note: This quilt has one pieced (Flying Geese) and five plain borders.

Fabric	Yardage	First Cut	Second Cut
Feature	2½ yards	6 strips 9½"	31 rectangles 6½" x 9½"
		3 strips 4¼"	24 squares 4¼" x 4¼" cut once diagonally to make 48 triangles
		1 strip 7¼"	4 squares 7¼" x 7¼"
		2 strips 3⅞"	12 squares 3⅞" x 3⅞"
Contrast	1 yard	2 strips 4¾"	12 squares 4¾" x 4¾"
		8 strips 2½" for 3rd border	
Coordinate	2¼ yards	6 strips 3½"	62 squares 3½" x 3½"
		8 strips 1¼" for 2nd border	
		8 strips 1¼" for 4th border	
		9 strips 3" for binding	
Background	4 yards	2 strips 9½"	18 rectangles 3½" x 9½"
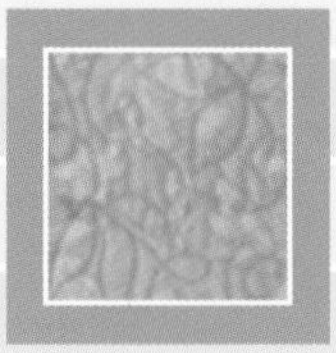		2 strips 6½"	18 rectangles 3½" x 6½"
		6 strips 3½"	62 squares 3½" x 3½"
		3 strips 3⅞"	28 squares 3⅞" x 3⅞"
		7 strips 3½" for 1st (inner) border	
		9 strips 5" for 5th (outer) border	
Backing	7⅜ yards		
Batting	84" x 99"		
Binding	See Coordinate		

*Drawings not to scale to show
technique and detail.*

Step 1

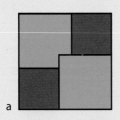

a

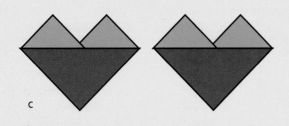

b

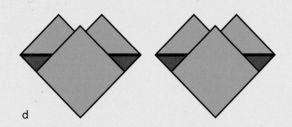

c

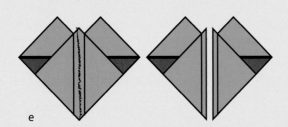

d

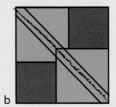

e

f

Step 1

From your fabrics select:

  4 feature 7¼" x 7¼" squares

  16 background 3⅞" x 3⅞" squares

Follow the pictures to make 16 Flying Geese. These should measure 3½" x 6½" when completed (finished size 3"x 6").

a) Place 2 background 3⅞" x 3⅞" squares right-sides down on 1 feature 7¼" x 7¼" square, diagonally opposite each other and overlapping in the middle.

b) Draw a line from corner to corner diagonally across the overlapping squares. Sew ¼" from each side of the line.

c) Cut on the drawn line. Separate the halves and press so the units look like hearts.

d) Place 1 more background square, right-side down, on each heart.

e) Draw a line from corner to corner on the newly added square. Sew ¼" from each side of that line. Cut on the drawn line.

f) Press to form 2 Flying Geese blocks. Repeat this process to make 16 Flying Geese blocks measuring 3½" x 6½". You will use 14 of them.

Step 2

Use: 12 contrast 4¾" x 4¾" squares

  48 feature triangles

Sew 2 feature triangles to opposite sides of 1 contrast square. Press the seams toward the triangles. Repeat on the remaining 2 sides of the square. Square-up and trim any excess background creating a 6½" square with ¼" seam allowance at the 4 points of the diamond.

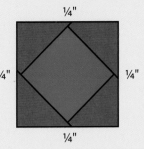

Step 2

Make 12

Step 3

Use: 12 background 3⅞" x 3⅞" squares

  12 feature 3⅞" x 3⅞" squares

Place 1 background square right-side down on 1 feature square. Using a pencil or chalk marker, draw a line diagonally from corner to corner. Sew ¼" on each side of the drawn line. Cut on the drawn line. Press the seam open and square the block to 3½".

Step 3

Make 24

Step 4

Use: 4 background 3½" x 3½" squares

  4 background 3½" x 6½" rectangles

  6 coordinate 3½" x 3½" squares

Make 2 blocks as shown. Press seams toward coordinate squares.

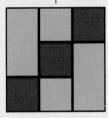

Step 4

Make 1   Make 1

Step 5

Use: 30 background 3½" x 3½" squares

  10 background 3½" x 6½" rectangles

  30 coordinate 3½" x 3½" squares

  10 feature/background 3½" Step 3 units

Sew these into 10 blocks as shown. Press the seams toward the coordinate 10 squares.

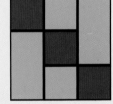

Step 5

Make 10

Step 6

Use: 18 coordinate 3½" x 3½" squares

  24 background 3½" x 3½" squares

  12 feature/background 3½" Step 3 units

Sew these into 6 blocks as shown. Press the seams toward the coordinate squares.

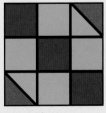

Step 6

Make 6

Step 7

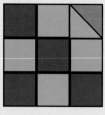

Make 2

Step 7

Use: 8 coordinate 3½" x 3½" squares
8 background 3½" x 3½" squares
2 HSTs of feature and background

Sew these into 2 blocks. Press seams toward the background squares

Step 8

To simplify assembly, place all of the sewn blocks and remaining pieces within reach. Sew the top together as follows:

Make 4 rows. Press the seams toward the feature rectangles.

Step 8

Make 4 rows

Make 1 row. Press the seams to the feature rectangles.

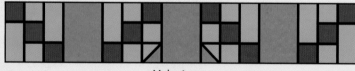

Make 1 row

Make 3 rows. Press the seams toward the feature rectangles.

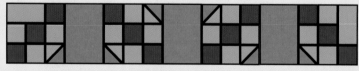

Make 3 rows

Make 1 row. Press the seams toward the feature rectangles.

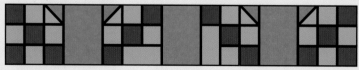

Make 1 row

Piece the top following the assembly diagram on page 53.

Step 9

To add the Flying Geese border use:

  14 Step 1 Flying Geese units

  18 background 3½" x 9½" rectangles

  4 coordinate 3½" x 3½" squares

Step 9

Make 2 rows

Make 2 rows

Make 2 rows. Press the seams away from the Flying Geese blocks.

Make 2 rows

Sew the side borders on first. Press the seams toward the borders. Then sew the top and bottom borders, matching the cornerstones to the side borders. Press the seams toward the borders.

Step 10

Attach borders 1 through 5, sides first, then top and bottom, in order.

Carefully measure across the center seams of the quilt, horizontally and vertically. This is the border strip length. Remeasure after each border addition to cut subsequent border strips.

For a perfect border fit, quarter the top and borders to create pin placement marks: fold each in half, crease, then in half again and crease. Use the crease marks as you pin raw edges together, starting at the center. If needed, ease in fullness within quarters.

Add the first border by squaring the top. Then measure through the quilt top center vertically to determine the side border length. Piece border strips together end-to-end if necessary, trim them to the desired length, and pin one to each side.

Assembly Diagram

WAY TO GO!

Repeat to add the top and bottom borders, measuring horizontally through the center of the quilt (which now includes the side borders).

Square the top again if necessary and repeat the measuring/piecing sequence to add the second, third, and fourth borders. Press and admire!!

You're ready to square the top, layer it with batting and backing, baste the layers, quilt as desired, and bind and label your quilt.

Simply Awesome Spaghetti Squash

1 medium spaghetti squash

1–2 T olive oil

2 medium onions, chopped

2–3 cloves garlic, minced

2 ribs celery, chopped

¾ cup zesty Italian dressing

½ cup shredded Parmesan cheese

Prick a clean, whole spaghetti squash with a sharp knife in several places. Place on a paper towel and microwave until done (10–15 minutes depending on squash size and microwave). Turn the squash over occasionally. Squash will begin to soften in the middle when done. Allow to sit and continue cooking while preparing remaining ingredients.

In a skillet over high heat, sauté onions, celery, and garlic in olive oil until they just begin to turn golden. Remove from heat. Cut squash in half lengthwise and scoop out seeds. Scrape the pulp into a large bowl, separating into spaghetti strands. Mix in sautéed veggies, tossing well. Pour into a greased casserole dish. Top with cheese and bake at 350 degrees, uncovered, about 10 minutes, or until cheese begins to brown.

Hint

When unsewing a seam, if you can find the bobbin side of the seam and get a thread-tail started, often you can gently tug and draw out quite a bit of thread before it breaks. Do this over and over and when the bobbin thread is all pulled out, just lift off the top thread.

Cabins in the Stars

78" x 90"

Girls Just Wanna Have Fun – or – Babes on a Boat

My brother has a lake house about three and a half hours from our shop. I take my staff there a couple of times a year, ostensibly for sewing retreats. Actually, very little sewing is accomplished! If the weather is warm, we just hang out in the lake.

One particularly hot afternoon twelve of us were floating lazily just off the dock in life jackets with rubber rafts and water noodles. Carol had forgotten her bathing suit, but I convinced her to try one of mine. She walked down to the lake in the borrowed suit, self-consciously attempting to cover up with a life jacket.

Unfortunately, she put the jacket on inside-out and struggled to zip it. We coaxed her into the water where she hunkered down in the shallows and pretended to enjoy herself. When a game of "squirt the girlfriends with the water noodle" broke out, Carol got out of the water, the suit looking much different. "Carol!" I called. "I didn't know that suit had a skirt!" She had self-consciously tugged it down to the point where it came to her knees. We were all relieved that she had managed to zip up that life jacket!

Yardage & Cutting

All strips are cut their measurement by 40" (width of fabric).

Fabric	Yardage	First Cut	Second Cut
Feature	3 yards	2 strips 6½"	10 squares 6½" x 6½"
		9 strips 6½" for outer border	
		9 strips 3" for binding	
Contrast	2 yards	3 strips 4½"	20 squares 4½" x 4½"
		2 strips 7¼"	10 squares 7¼" x 7¼"
		4 strips 3½"	40 squares 3½" x 3½"
		7 strips 3½" for inner border	
Coordinate	2 yards	20 strips 2½" for dark logs	
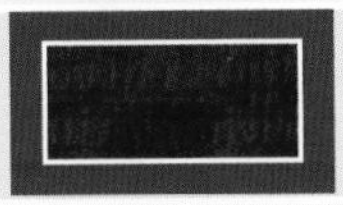		4 strips 3⅞"	40 squares 3⅞" x 3⅞" for star points
Background	1⅔ yards	20 strips 2½" for light logs	
Backing	7⅝ yards		
Batting	86" x 98"		
Binding	See feature		

Drawings not to scale to show technique and detail.

Step 1

a

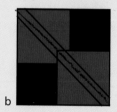
b

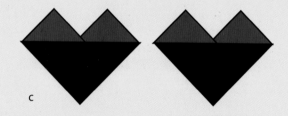
c

d

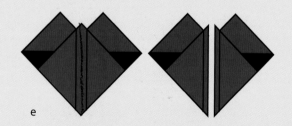
e

f

Step 1

From your fabrics select:

    10 contrast 7¼" x 7¼" squares

    40 coordinate 3⅞" x 3⅞" squares.

Follow the pictures step-by-step until you complete 40 Flying Geese blocks. They should measure 3½"x 6½".

a) Place 2 coordinate 3⅞" x 3⅞" squares right-sides down on 1 contrast 7¼" x 7¼" square, diagonally opposite each other and overlapping in the middle.

b) Draw a line from corner to corner diagonally across the overlapping squares. Sew ¼" from each side of the line.

c) Cut on the drawn line. Separate the halves and press so the units look like hearts.

d) Place 1 more coordinate square, right-side down, on each heart.

e) Draw a line from corner to corner on the newly added square. Sew ¼" from each side of that line. Cut on the drawn line.

f) Press to form 2 Flying Geese blocks. Repeat this process to make 40 Flying Geese blocks measuring 3½" x 6½".

Step 2

Assemble the Flying Geese, 6½" squares of feature fabric, and 3½" squares of contrast fabric into 10 Star blocks. Press.

Step 3

Create the Log Cabin blocks with assembly-line piecing: place 1 contrast 4½" square right-side down on the right side of 1 background 2½" strip. Sew as shown. Butt the next contrast 4½" square up to the one just sewn and repeat. Continue until there is no more room on the background strip for another 4½" square. Take another background strip and continue until all the 4½" contrast squares have been sewn to background strips. Cut blocks apart and press the seams away from the contrast squares. *These blocks will be more accurate if sewn with a scant ¼" seam.*

Step 4

Turn the block so the background strip runs across the top. Place it right-sides together on another 2½" strip of background and sew as before, butting each unit up to the next and continuing to sew to the end of the strip. Use new background strips as needed. When all Step 3 units have been sewn to the second set of background strips, cut them apart and press the seam toward the newly added background strip.

Step 5

Continuing as before, but now using a 2½" strip of coordinate fabric, keep the most recently added background strip to the top, place the growing block right-sides-together with the coordinate fabric and sew, butting each new block up to the last. Use more coordinate strips as needed until all blocks have been sewn. Cut apart and press seams to the newest strip.

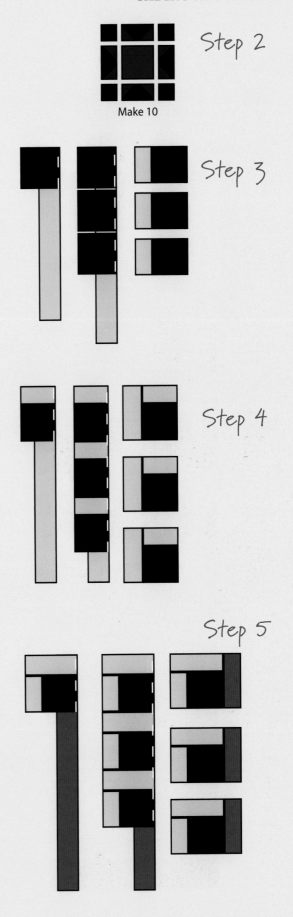

Step 2

Make 10

Step 3

Step 4

Step 5

Step 6

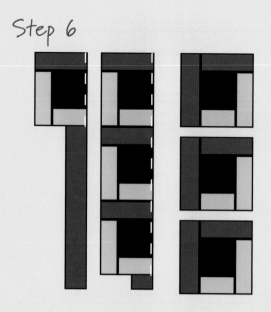

Step 6

Continue using the coordinate fabric strips, turn the most recently added strip to the top, place blocks right-sides down on the new coordinate strip, and sew, trim, and press as before.

Step 7

Now go back to using the background strips. Again, turn the growing block so that the most recently added strip is across the top and right-sides together with the background strip and sew the blocks:

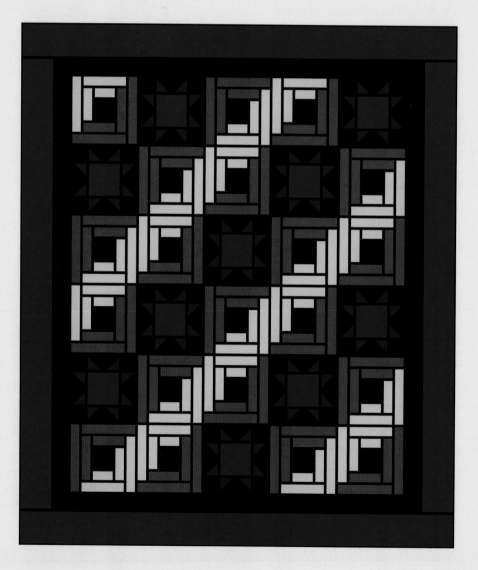

Step 8

Finish the Log Cabin block with three more rounds: use another background strip; then switch to using a coordinate strip for 2 more rounds. Follow the quilt photo on page 56 to be sure you place each round correctly.

Step 9

Follow the quilt photo to assemble the top, laying out the rows of Star and Log Cabin blocks. Sew one row at a time, pressing the seams in one direction. Try to press each row's seams in opposite directions. After all of the rows are sewn, join them to each other. Press.

Step 10

Carefully measure across the center seams of the quilt, horizontally and vertically. (If they are not the same measurement, pick the average.) This is the border strip length. Remeasure after each border addition to cut subsequent border strips.

For a perfect border fit, quarter the top and borders to create pin placement marks: fold each in half, crease, then in half again and crease. Use the crease marks as you pin raw edges together, starting at the center. If needed, ease in fullness within quarters.

Add the inner border by first squaring the top. Then measure through the quilt top center vertically to determine the side border length. Piece border strips together end-to-end if necessary, trim them to the desired length, and pin one to each side.

Repeat to add the top and bottom borders, measuring horizontally through the center of the quilt (which now includes the side borders).

Square the top again if necessary and repeat the measuring/piecing sequence to add the outer border. Press and admire!!

You're ready to square the top, layer it with batting and backing, baste the layers, quilt as desired, and bind and label your quilt.

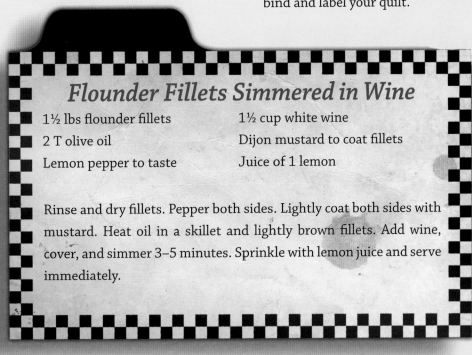

Flounder Fillets Simmered in Wine

1½ lbs flounder fillets

2 T olive oil

Lemon pepper to taste

1½ cup white wine

Dijon mustard to coat fillets

Juice of 1 lemon

Rinse and dry fillets. Pepper both sides. Lightly coat both sides with mustard. Heat oil in a skillet and lightly brown fillets. Add wine, cover, and simmer 3–5 minutes. Sprinkle with lemon juice and serve immediately.

Sawtooth Patchwork Irish Chain

95" x 119"

The Money Pit – or – Seeing the Light

It had always been my dream to own an historic home. Well, as the sages say, "Be careful what you wish for." We bought a nineteenth-century Georgian-style funeral home for our ever-growing quilt shop. It was a beauty and it was ours! Also ours were the repair bills for upgraded electric, better lighting, replaced plumbing, new roof, and on and on. Despite the financial drain, we have a huge affection for our shop. We consider her a comforting good friend with years of experience. One afternoon the former owner stopped by to see what we had done. I proudly showed off the wonderful, clear lighting that allowed us to see the true colors of our luscious fabrics. He stood for a moment in the middle of what had been one of the viewing rooms, looked around and said, "Well, you see, we really didn't want to have this clear, bright light in our business."

Yardage & Cutting

All strips are cut their measurement by 40" (width of fabric).

Fabric	Yardage	First Cut	Second Cut
Feature	5½ yards	5 strips 9½"	17 squares 9½" x 9½"
		6 strips 3½"	66 squares 3½" x 3½" + 2 from 9½" scraps
		11 strips 7½" for outer border	
		12 strips 3" for binding	
Contrast	1⅓ yards	3 strips 8¾"	33 rectangles 3½" x 8¾" + 1 from 17" scraps
		1 strip 17"	3 rectangles 17"x 11½"
Coordinate	2 yards	17 strips 3½"	180 squares 3½" x 3½"
		9 strips 1¼" for middle border	
Background	4½ yards	4 strips 9½"	14 squares 9½" x 9½"
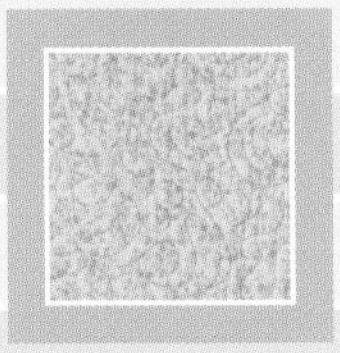		4 strips 3½"	42 squares 3½" x 3½"
		3 strips 8¾"	33 rectangles 3½" x 8¾" + 1 from 17" scraps
		1 strip 17"	3 rectangles 17" x 11½"
		3 strips 6½"	28 rectangles 3½" x 6½"
		4 strips 4"	34 squares 4" x 4"
		9 strips 2¾" for inner border	
Backing	10½ yards	(3 pieces 126" long)	
Batting	103" x 127"		
Binding	See feature		

OTHER SUPPLIES

34 sheets 3" Thangles™
3 sheets 3" Quarter-Square Triangle Paper

Step 1

Make 136

Step 1

Make half-square triangles with:

34 sheets of 3" Thangles

   34 background 3½" x 8¾" rectangles

   34 contrast 3½" x 8¾" rectangles

Place 1 background rectangle right-sides together on 1 contrast rectangle. Pin 1 sheet of Thangles to this strip-pair. Shorten the machine stitch length to about 1.5. Sew on all the dotted lines. Cut on all the solid lines. Carefully tear away the paper.

Press the seam open. When all background and contrast rectangles have been sewn to the Thangles paper and pressed, you should have 136 half-square triangles. Set these aside.

Snips

If I quilt fast enough, does it count as aerobic exercise? – Author Unknown

Step 2

Make quarter-square triangles using:

3 sheets of 3" Quarter-Square Triangle Paper

   3 background 17" x 11½" rectangles

   3 contrast 17" x 11½" rectangles

As in Step 1, place the fabrics right-sides together and pin the triangle sheet to the fabrics. Shorten the stitch length, sew on all the dotted lines, cut on all the solid lines, tear away the paper, and press seams open. (You will have a few left over.)

Step 2

Make 68

Step 3

Cut the 34 background 4" x 4" squares in half once diagonally.

Place 1 of these triangles right-sides together on each of the Step 2 units. Sew across the widest side of the triangle pair. Press the seam open.

Step 3

Make 68

Step 4

Sew together in 4 blocks:

    8 background 3½" x 6½" rectangles

    12 coordinate 3½" x 3½" squares

    8 background 3½" x 3½" squares

Press the seams toward the dark squares. Press horizontal seams in one direction.

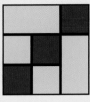

Step 4

Make 4

Step 5

Sew together into 10 blocks:

    10 Step 3 units

    20 Step 1 units

    50 coordinate 3½" x 3½" squares

    20 background 3½"x 6½" rectangles

    20 background 3½" x 3½" squares

    10 feature 3½" x 3½" squares

Press seams toward the darker fabric in the horizontal rows (and toward the feature fabric). Press horizontal seams down.

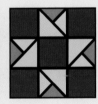

Step 5

Make 10

Step 6

Sew together in 3 different Nine-Patch blocks:

    90 coordinate 3½" x 3½" squares

    14 background 3½" x 3½" squares

    58 Step 3 units

Press all vertical seams toward the coordinate fabric. Press horizontal seams in one direction.

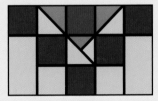

Step 6

Make 4   Make 6   Make 8

Step 7

Sew together into 17 blocks:

    17 feature 9½" x 9½" squares

    34 feature 3½" x 3½" squares

    68 Step 1 half-square triangles

Press seams toward the feature square.

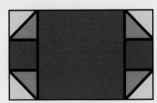

Step 7

Make 17

Step 8

From the pieces remaining, sew 6 blocks. (You will still have pieces leftover.) Note: You are building this block around 6 of the Step 6 Nine-Patches. Press horizontal rows toward coordinate and feature fabrics. Press horizontal seams in one direction.

Step 8

Make 6

Step 9

Place the finished blocks in separate piles. You will have 14 background 9½" x 9½" squares and 4 coordinate 3½" x 3½" squares remaining.

Following the quilt photo, lay out all of the blocks. (The easiest way is row-by-row.) Begin the first row with the upper left Step 4 background-and-coordinate block. Start the second row with a remaining 9½" background square. The third row starts with a Step 5 block. Continue by repeating rows 2 and 3. Refer to the assembly diagram. Press row seams in alternate directions. Each horizontal row can be pressed in any direction.

Step 10

Border 1 is a double border*. Begin by sewing the 9 background 2¾" strips end-to-end into one long strip. Press seams open. Repeat this process with the 9 coordinate 1¼" strips. After pressing seams open, sew both of these strips together, long sides togeth-

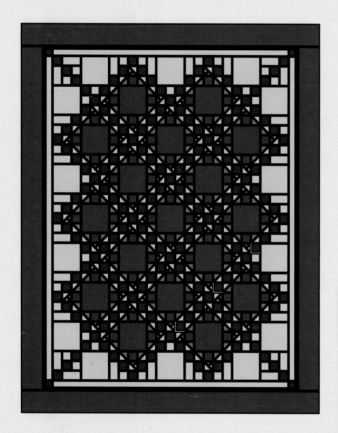

er. Press the seams toward the coordinate fabric. *The strips most likely will not be the same length.

Measure the pieced quilt top horizontally and vertically through the center. Cut 2 strip-pairs the horizontal measurement length, and 2 strip-pairs the vertical measurement length.

For a perfect border fit, quarter the top and borders to create pin placement marks: fold each in half, crease, then in half again and crease. Use the crease marks as you pin raw edges together, starting at the center. If needed, ease in fullness within quarters. Press the seam toward the border.

After quartering the top and bottom borders, sew one 3½" coordinate square to each end of these 2

borders. Matching these coordinate squares to the borders already on your quilt, and matching your quarter marks on the borders and on the quilt, sew the top and bottom borders to your quilt. Press the seams toward the new borders.

For border 2 sew the 7½" feature strips end-to-end. Press the seams open. Measure the top, cut the strips to length, and quarter the top and border. Sew this new border down one long side of the quilt. Press the seam to this border and square-up both ends with the quilt. This will prevent your borders from stretching and distorting. Repeat this with the other border, and then add the top and bottom borders. Admire your beautiful quilt!!

You're ready to square the top, layer it with batting and backing, baste the layers, quilt as desired, and bind and label your quilt.

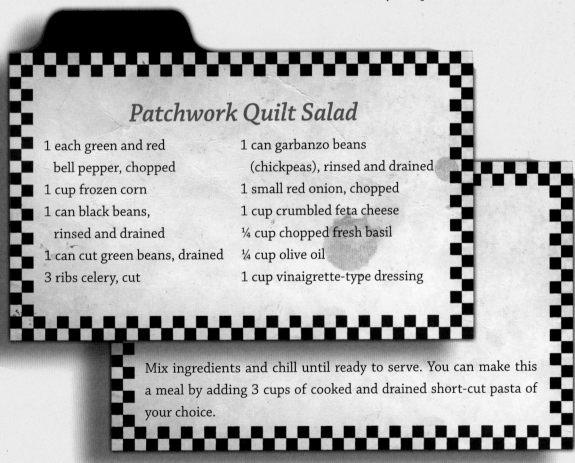

Patchwork Quilt Salad

1 each green and red
  bell pepper, chopped
1 cup frozen corn
1 can black beans,
  rinsed and drained
1 can cut green beans, drained
3 ribs celery, cut

1 can garbanzo beans
  (chickpeas), rinsed and drained
1 small red onion, chopped
1 cup crumbled feta cheese
¼ cup chopped fresh basil
¼ cup olive oil
1 cup vinaigrette-type dressing

Mix ingredients and chill until ready to serve. You can make this a meal by adding 3 cups of cooked and drained short-cut pasta of your choice.

Sedona Stones

103" x 93"

Hint

If you have good scissors that you really don't want anyone else using, purchase a small padlock and lock the handles closed. Keep the key in the tray of your sewing machine.

Rock On! – or –
Did You Say Something to Me?

It was February and time to plan my annual teaching trip to Ajo, Arizona, in the extreme southwestern part of the state, and then visit friends in Phoenix, Flagstaff, and several other cities.

In my weekly e-letter to customers and friends, I mentioned that we would be staying in Sedona for several days. This prompted a reply from a customer/friend who had just returned from there. She wrote that I really should take the time to go to the Bell Rock for a hot stone message. Hmmm.

I know Sedona is known for its New Age visionaries and vortexes and such, but I never knew my friend got messages from rocks, regardless of temperature or location.

Feeling very New-Age spiritual, I replied to her e-mail saying I would do my best to keep my ears open and mind receptive to messages at the Bell Rock. Just before I hit the "send" button I re-read her letter, and then my reply. She had not been listening to rocks after all. She had gotten a hot stone massage! Aha. I rewrote my answer.

Yardage & Cutting

All strips are cut their measurement by 40" (width of fabric).

Fabric	Yardage	First Cut	Second Cut
Feature	4¾ yards	10 strips 6½"	56 squares 6½" x 6½"
		10 strips 7" for outer border	
		10 strips 3" for binding	
Coordinate	2½ yards	14 strips 2½"	224 squares 2½" x 2½"
		17 strips 2½" for 1st and 3rd borders	
Contrast	1¼ yards	14 strips 2½"	224 squares 2½" x 2½"
Background	2⅔ yards		
		8 strips 2½"	116 squares 2½" x 2½"
		7 strips 6½"	112 rectangles 2½" x 6½"
		9 strips 1½" for 2nd border	
Backing	8⅞ yards	3 strips 101"	
Batting	111" x 101"		
Binding	See feature		

Step 1

Make 112

Step 2

Make 56

Step 3

Make 28

Step 4

Block A
Make 28

Step 5

Make 28

Step 6

Make 56

Step 7

Block B
Make 28

Step 1

Use: 112 background 2½" x 2½" squares

224 contrast 2½" x 2½" squares

Sew 2 contrast squares to opposite sides of each background square. Press the seams in one direction.

Step 2

Use: 56 Step 1 units

112 coordinate 2½" x 2½" squares

Sew 1 coordinate square to each end of a Step 1 unit.

Step 3

Use: 28 feature 6½" x 6½" squares

56 Step 1 units

Sew a Step 1 unit to opposite sides of a feature square. Press seams toward the square.

Step 4

Sew a Step 2 unit to opposite sides of the Step 3 units. Press seams toward the square.

Step 5

Use: 28 feature 6½" x 6½" squares

56 background 2½" x 6½" rectangles

Sew a background rectangle to opposite sides of a feature square. Press seams toward the square.

Step 6

Use: 56 background 2½" x 6½" rectangles

112 coordinate 2½" x 2½" squares

Sew a coordinate square to opposite ends of a rectangle. Press seams toward the rectangle.

Step 7

Sew a Step 6 unit to the top and bottom of each Step 5 unit. Press seams toward the newly added units.

Step 8

Make 7 rows of alternating Blocks A and B. Start 4 rows with Block A and 3 rows with Block B.

Step 8

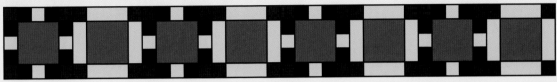

Make 7

Step 9

Referring to the assembly diagram, sew the top, flipping alternate rows. Note that the quilt is wider than it is long.

Snips

Every quilt is a self-portrait of the quilter who made it.

Step 10

Sew all 17 coordinate 2½" strips end-to-end. Press seams open. Square the quilt top.

Measure through the quilt top center vertically and horizontally. Cut 2 border strips for each measurement.

For a perfect border fit, quarter the top and borders to create pin placement marks: fold each in half, crease, then in half again and crease. Use the crease marks as you pin raw edges together, starting at the center. If needed, ease in fullness within quarters.

Sew 2 borders to the sides of the quilt. Press the seams toward the border.

Sew 1 background 2½" x 2½" square to each end of the remaining 2 border strips. Press the seams away from the cornerstones. Quarter the top and bottom of the quilt and do the same to the borders. Pin and sew. Note: You will need to match the cornerstones to the lengthwise borders already sewn to your quilt. Press the seams toward the border.

Square the top again if necessary and repeat the measuring/piecing sequence to add the remaining borders. Press and admire!!

You're ready to square the top, layer it with batting and backing, baste the layers, quilt as desired, and bind and label your quilt.

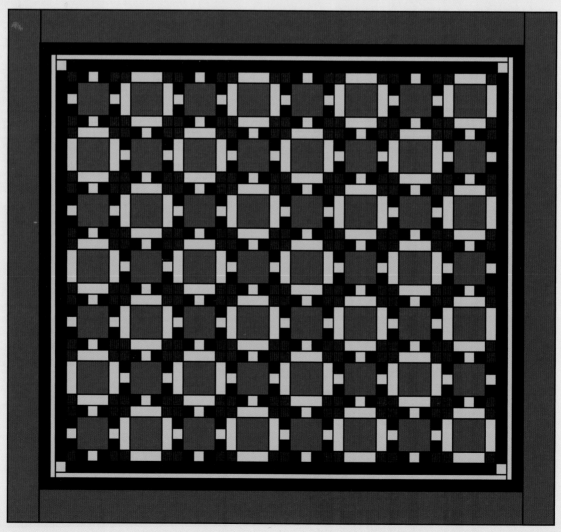

Southwestern Salsa Swiss Steak

1 T olive oil

1½ lbs boneless beef
  top round steak

2 onions, chunked

1 can cream of mushroom soup w/garlic

1 cup chunky salsa

Trim fat from steak and cut into 4 serving pieces. Heat oil in large skillet. Sauté beef and onion for about 5 minutes or until browned, turning once. Place in 4–6 quart slow cooker. In the same skillet, combine soup and salsa and mix well with drippings. Pour over steak in crockpot. Cover and cook on LOW setting for 8–10 hours. 4 servings.

Mexican Confetti Dip

1 12 oz can whole kernel corn, drained

1 15 oz can black beans, rinsed and drained

1/3 cup fat-free Italian salad dressing

1 16 oz jar chunky salsa

Mix all together and chill. Serve with tortilla chips and maybe some sour cream. Ole!

Hint

"When things go wrong as they sometimes will;

When the road you're trudging seems all uphill;

When the funds are low and the debts are high;

And you want to smile but you have to sigh;

When care is pressing you down a bit,

Rest if you must but never quit." Anonymous

Stars at Sea

92" x 104"

Her Just Dessert – or –
Do Cruise Calories Really Count?

It was our first cruise and we planned to experience it all! One afternoon Charlotte and I visited the dessert bar. Tasty treats and caloric morsels vying for attention, she ended up with two full plates! Balancing her array of sweets with both hands as we chatted and laughed our way to the deck, Charlotte turned to speak to me and ran into the wet-floor caution cone. She sprawled flat and both plates sailed across the deck! I was laughing too hard to help, but several guests came to her aid. While the deck steward tended to the mess, Charlotte walked back into the dining room, returning with two identical plates full of sweets. She said, "The dessert bar hostess was amazed that I finished all my goodies so quickly!"

Yardage & Cutting

All strips are cut their measurement by 40" (width of fabric).

Fabric	Yardage	First Cut	Second Cut
Feature	4¾ yards	4 strips 6½"	21 squares 6½" x 6½"
		11 strips 4½"	84 squares 4½" x 4½"
		10 strips 5½" strips for outer border	
		10 strips 3" for binding	
Contrast	2¾ yards	5 strips 7¼"	21 squares 7¼" x 7¼"
		8 strips 3½"	84 squares 3½" x 3½"
		11 strips 2½"	168 squares 2½" x 2½"
Background	3 yards	3 strips 4½"	21 squares 4½" x 4½"
		9 strips 3⅞"	84 squares 3⅞" x 3⅞" + 4 squares 3½" x 3½" for border cornerstones
		11 strips 2½"	168 squares 2½" x 2½"
		9 strips 2½" for middle border	
Zinger 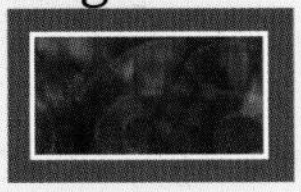	⅞ yard	8 strips 3½" for inner border	
Backing	8⅞ yards		
Batting	100" x 112"		
Binding	See feature		

Drawings not to scale to show technique and detail.

Step 1

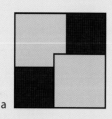

a

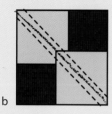

b

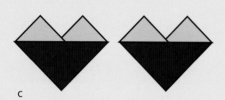

c

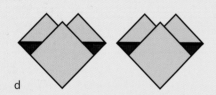

d

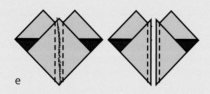

e

f

Step 1

From your fabric select

21 contrast 7¼" x 7¼" squares

84 background 3⅞" x 3⅞" squares

Follow the pictures step-by-step until you complete 84 Flying Geese blocks. They should measure 3½" x 6½".

a) Place 2 background 3⅞" x 3⅞" squares right-sides down on 1 contrast 7¼" x 7¼" square, diagonally opposite each other and overlapping in the middle.

b) Draw a line from corner to corner diagonally across the overlapping squares. Sew ¼" from each side of the line.

c) Cut on the drawn line. Separate the halves and press so the units look like hearts.

d) Place 1 more background square right-side down on each heart.

e) Draw a line from corner to corner on the newly added square. Sew ¼" from each side of that line. Cut on the drawn line.

f) Press to form 2 Flying Geese blocks. Repeat this process to make 84 Flying Geese blocks measuring 3½" x 6½".

Step 2

Create 21 Star blocks using the Step 1 Flying Geese blocks plus:

   84 contrast 3½" x 3½" squares
   21 feature 6½" x 6½" squares

Assemble the blocks as Nine-Patch units. Press well.

Step 2

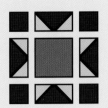

Step 3

Sew the 168 background 2½" x 2½" squares and 168 contrast 2½" x 2½" squares into pairs. Press the seam toward the contrast square.

Step 3

Make 168

Step 4

Sew the Step 3 units into Four-Patch blocks. Press the seams in any direction.

Step 4

Make 84

Step 5

Sew the 84 Step 4 Four-Patch blocks, the 84 feature 4½" x 4½" squares, and the 21 background 4½" x 4½" squares into 21 blocks. Press all seams toward the feature blocks.

Step 5

Make 21

Step 6

Sew the Step 2 and Step 5 blocks into 7 rows. Begin 4 rows with Step 5 blocks and 3 rows with Step 2 blocks so the rows alternate. Press seams away from the Star blocks.

Step 6

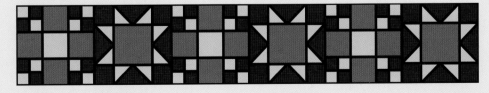

Step 7

Sew the 7 rows together, alternating them. Press well.

Step 8

Carefully measure across the vertical center seams of the quilt. Cut 2 border strips this length for the long sides of the top.

For a perfect border fit, quarter the top and borders to create pin placement marks: fold each in half, crease, then in half again and crease. Use the crease marks as you pin raw edges together, starting at the center. If needed, ease in fullness within quarters. Press seams toward new borders.

Now measure across the center of the quilt horizontally to include the side borders. Cut 2 border strips this length. Sew them to the top and bottom of the quilt top. Press seams toward new borders.

Sew the 8 zinger 3½" strips end-to-end. Cut 2 strips to the vertical border measurement and sew them to the sides of the quilt top. Press the seams toward the border.

Sew the 4 background 3½" x 3½" squares to each end of the remaining 2 strips of zinger border. Add the border to the top and to the bottom of the quilt. Press the seams away from the cornerstones.

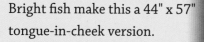

Bright fish make this a 44" x 57" tongue-in-cheek version.

Add the second border using the 9 background 2½" strips, measuring, sewing end-to-end, and matching cornerstones to the already-sewn border seams. Press and square the corners.

Add the outer border using the 5½" feature strips. Press well and admire!!

You're ready to square the top, layer it with batting and backing, baste the layers, quilt as desired, and bind and label your quilt.

Rita's Guilt-Free (Sugarless) Apple Pie

6 Granny Smith apples, peeled, cored, chunked
and tossed with 3 T lemon juice
½ cup raisins or cranberry raisins
¼ cup undiluted apple juice concentrate
2 T cinnamon + extra for sprinkling
2 T butter
3 T cornstarch
Unbaked pie shell and top crust (recipe below)

In a saucepan heat the undiluted apple juice, butter, and cornstarch. Cook over medium-high heat, stirring constantly until it begins to thicken. Pour over the apples. Add raisins and 2 tablespoons of cinnamon. Gently blend all together and pour into unbaked pie shell. Place the top crust onto the pie, crimp the edges, and slit steam holes into the top with a sharp knife. Sprinkle with extra cinnamon. Bake at 450 degrees for 20 minutes. Reduce to 375 degrees and continue to bake until filling bubbles and pie crust is golden (about 45–60 minutes).

Pie Shell and Top Crust

2 cups flour   ⅔ cup canola or vegetable oil
1 t salt   ¼ cup water or juice

Combine ingredients in a large bowl. Stir gently with a fork. (Don't overwork the dough.) Pat dough into a round ball. Separate ⅔ of dough. Roll this out between 2 sheets of waxed paper. Place shell in pie pan. Roll remaining ⅓ dough for top crust.

Duck Feet

42" x 42"

Hint

When you are into a large project requiring multiple bobbins, store the extras on your machine's second spool pin. They are ready to grab-and-go in a jiffy!

Old McRonald Had a Farm – or – Life's Just Ducky on the Funny Farm

One Mother's Day my kids presented me with two abandoned ducklings we named Stack 'n Quack. Sadly, after a few weeks, one died, but the bereaved Stack (or Quack) thrived and continued to get bigger and bigger. One evening as our daughter Shannon and I were doing dishes and watching Stack (or Quack) through the kitchen window, she said, "Mom, are you looking at that duck?" I said, "Yes." "Well, she's not a duck, she's a goose." Ha! That sure explained her weight problem!

Several weeks later, I took Stack (or Honk) to the park to release her. I sat on top of the carrier and watched the lake as I waited for Stack (or Honk) to decide to leave the safety of her box. A prison work crew man walked past picking up litter and said, "Good morning, ma'am." I replied that I was offering my goose her freedom, but she didn't quite know what to do with it. He said, "Yes ma'am. I know what that's like."

Yardage & Cutting

All strips are cut their measurement by 40" (width of fabric).

Fabric	Yardage	First Cut	Second Cut
Red	¾ yard	2 strips 2⅞"	16 squares 2⅞" x 2⅞"
		1 strip 4⅞"	2 squares 4⅞" x 4⅞" + 4 squares 4½" x 4½"
		4 strips 3½" for outer border	
Black & white	¾ yard	1 strip 4½"	8 squares 4½" x 4½"
		1 strip 9¼"	1 square 9¼" x 9¼" + 4 rectangles 4½"x 8½" + 4 squares 2" x 2"
		1 strip 2½"	8 squares 2½" x 2½"
		1 strip 3½"	4 squares 3½" x 3½" for cornerstones
		4 strips 1¼" for middle border	
Black solid	1¼ yards	1 strip 5¼"	4 squares 5¼" x 5¼" + 8 squares 2½" x 2½"
		2 strips 4⅞"	14 squares 4⅞" x 4⅞"
		1 strip 4½"	4 squares 4½" x 4½"
		4 strips 2" for inner border	
		4 strips 3" for binding	
White	½ yard	1 strip 9¼"	2 squares 9¼" x 9¼"
		1 strip 4½"	8 squares 4½" x 4½"
Backing	3 yards		
Batting	50" x 50"		
Binding	See black solid		

DUCK FEET

Step 1

Drawings not to scale to show technique and detail.

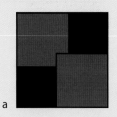

a

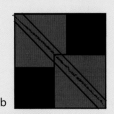

b

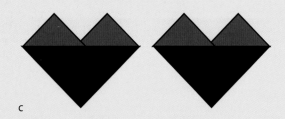

c

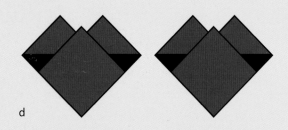

d

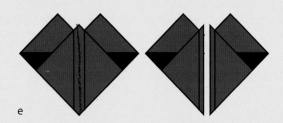

e

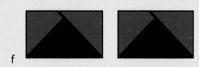

f

Step 1

From your fabrics select:

    4 black 5¼" x 5¼" squares

    16 red 2⅞" x 2⅞" squares

Follow the pictures step-by-step until you complete 16 Flying Geese blocks. They should measure 2½" x 4½".

a) Place 2 red 2⅞" x 2⅞" squares right-sides down on 1 black 5¼" x 5¼"square, diagonally opposite each other and overlapping in the middle.

b) Draw a line from corner to corner diagonally across the overlapping squares. Sew ¼" from each side of the line.

c) Cut on the drawn line. Separate the halves and press so the units look like hearts.

d) Place 1 more red square right-side down on each heart.

e) Draw a line from corner to corner on the newly added square. Sew ¼" from each side of that line. Cut on the drawn line.

f) Press to form 2 Flying Geese blocks. Repeat this process to make 16 Flying Geese blocks measuring 2½" x 4½".

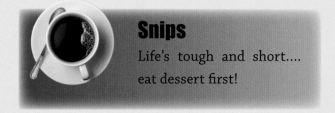

Snips

Life's tough and short.... eat dessert first!

Step 2

Create 4 Star blocks using the 16 Step 1 Flying Geese blocks plus:

    4 black-and-white 4½" x 4½" squares

    8 black 2½" x 2½" squares

    8 black-and-white 2½" x 2½" squares

Assemble the blocks as Nine-Patch units. When the Star block is complete, press the top and bottom seams toward the center square. The block should measure 8½" x 8½".

Step 3

Following Step 1, make 8 Flying Geese. You will use 2 white 9¼" x 9¼" squares and 8 black 4⅞" x 4⅞" squares. These blocks will measure 4½" x 8½".

Step 4

Following Step 1, make 4 Flying Geese. You will use 1 black-and-white 9¼" x 9¼" square and 4 black squares 4⅞" x 4⅞". These blocks will measure 4½" x 8½".

Step 5

Make 4 Flying Geese a different way:

Place 1 black 4½" x 4½" square right-side down in the right hand corner of 1 black-and-white 4½" x 8½" rectangle. Draw a line from corner to corner. Sew on the drawn line.

Trim away ¼" above the seam. Press the newly added triangle up to form a rectangle.

Repeat the place-draw-sew-trim-press sequence with 1 red 4½" x 4½" square on the opposite corner.

Make 4 Flying Geese that measure 4½" x 8½".

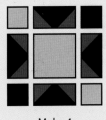

Step 2

Make 4

Hint

For a perfect border fit, quarter the top and borders to create pin placement marks: fold each in half, crease, then in half again and crease. Use the crease marks as you pin raw edges together, starting at the center. If needed, ease in fullness within quarters.

Step 5

Step 6

Make 4

Step 6

Place 2 red 4⅞" x 4⅞" squares right-sides together on 2 black 4⅞" x 4⅞" squares. Using a pencil or chalk marker, draw a diagonal line across each pair from corner to corner. Sew ¼" on each side of the drawn line. Cut on the drawn line. Press the seam open. Square up each of the 4 resulting half-square triangle blocks to 4½" x 4½".

Step 7

Make 4 Exploding Star blocks from: the Step 2 Star blocks; the Flying Geese blocks from Steps 3, 4, and 5; 4 black-and-white 4½" x 4½" squares; 8 white 4½" x 4½" squares, and 4 black-and-red half-square triangles from Step 6.

Assemble the blocks as Nine-Patches and press seams toward the center.

Step 7

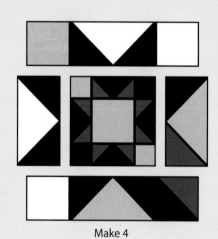

Make 4

Step 8

Sew the 4 finished blocks together as shown. The top should measure 32½" x 32½".

Step 8

Hint

It cannot be stressed enough: For best results in your quilting adventures, take the time to press-as-you-go!

Step 9

Carefully measure across the center seams of your quilt, horizontally and vertically. If they are not the same measurement, pick the average. Cut the 4 black 2" strips to that measurement.

For a perfect border fit, quarter the top and borders to create pin placement marks: fold each in half, crease, then in half again and crease. Use the crease marks as you pin raw edges together, starting at the center. If needed, ease in fullness within quarters. Press the seams toward the border.

Sew the 4 black-and-white 2" x 2" squares to each end of the remaining 2 strips of black border. Quar-

ter and add the border to the top and to the bottom of the quilt. Press the seams to the newly added border.

Add the second border using the 1¼" strips of black-and-white fabric. Press and square the corners.

Add the outer red border with the 4 black-and-white 3½" x 3½" cornerstones in the same manner as you did the first border. Press well when done and admire!

You're ready to square the top, layer it with batting and backing, baste the layers, quilt as desired, and bind and label your quilt.

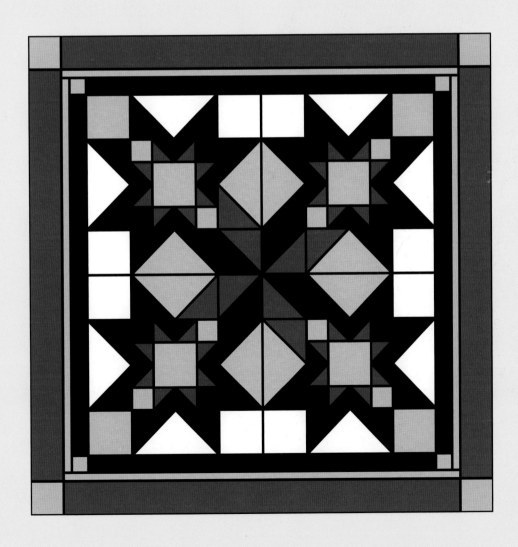

Ajo Star

68" x 68"

Follow the Star – or – Which Way? That-a-Way!

I was headed to charming Ajo, Arizona, where I'd be teaching a workshop for the next three days. I was not familiar with the route, nor the navigation helper, Tom-Tom, which my staff had given me as a Christmas present in hopes of saving me from my directionally-challenged self. I programmed Tom and confidently sped off. I had written directions from my host and thus ignored Tom's insistent "Turn around when possible." I was beginning to understand my friend's nickname for her GPS unit—The Nagigator.

Certain that Tom simply wasn't up-to-speed on the new highways outside of greater Phoenix, I continued to ignore him. I ignored him until I began to see exit signs for California. Really? Just as I realized I had made a BIG mistake in ignoring Mr. Tom, he must have had enough. As I picked him up to pay closer attention to his unrelenting demands, he ran out of battery and died—right in the middle of the Arizona desert.

Yardage & Cutting

All strips are cut their measurement by 40" (width of fabric).

Fabric	Yardage	First Cut	Second Cut
P (Feature)	3 yards	4 strips 3⅞"	36 squares 3⅞" x 3⅞"
		7 strips 6½" for outer border	
		7 strips 3" for binding	
B (Contrast)	¾ yard	3 strips 3⅞"	28 squares 3⅞" x 3⅞"
		6 strips 1½" for inner border	
A (Background)	1¼ yards	4 strips 3⅞"	40 squares 3⅞" x 3⅞"
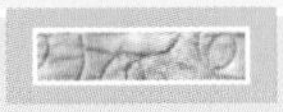		4 strips 3½"	4 rectangles 3½" x 24½"
T (Dark Coordinate) 	½ yard	3 strips 3⅞"	24 squares 3⅞" x 3⅞"
D (Dark Seafoam)	½ yard	3 strips 3⅞"	24 squares 3⅞" x 3⅞"
S (Seafoam)	1 yard	4 strips 3⅞"	36 squares 3⅞" x 3⅞"
		2 strips 2½"	16 squares 3½" x 3½"
R (Red) 	1½ yards	4 strips 3 7/8"	32 squares 3⅞" x 3⅞" + 1 square 3½" x 3½"
		1 strip 3½"	11 squares 3½" x 3½"
		1 strip 3½"	4 rectangles 3½" x 9½"
		2 strips 3½"	4 rectangles 3½" x 12½"
Binding	⅔ yard		
Batting	76"x 76"		
Backing	4½ yards		

Note: This yardage is generous enough to allow the use of half-square triangle-making paper if you prefer that method.

Making this quilt will be much easier if you first label your fabrics in the following manner:

Feature: P (Purple) – 3 yards

Contrast: B (Blue) – ¾ yard

Background: A (Aqua) – 1¼ yards

Dark coordinate: T (Teal) – ½ yard

Light coordinate: D (Dk Seafoam) – ½ yard

Main coordinate: S (Seafoam) – 1 yard

Zinger: R (Red) – 1½ yards

Binding: ⅔ yard

Batting: 76"x 76"

Backing: 4½ yards

These letters will make it easier for you to identify the placement as you compare the letters on your fabrics to the colors on the graph. Use a sheet of paper and tape swatches of fabric next to their respective letter.

Snips

A study years back discovered that women who sew experience a significant drop in heart rate, blood pressure, and perspiration rate compared to women who participate in other leisure activities. So when you're on pins and needles, pick up your pins and needles!

Hint

When ease-stitching a shorter piece of fabric to a longer piece, such as unmatched quilt blocks, sew with the longer piece against the feed dogs, then put a bit more tension on the top fabric as you sew them together.

Step 1

Make the half-square triangle (HST) combinations. Cut fabric squares 3⅞" x 3⅞". Place pairs right-sides together. Mark a diagonal line across one square and sew ¼" from each side of the line. Cut on the drawn line. Press the seam open. The block should measure 3½" x 3½".* You will get 2 HST blocks from every sewn pair of 3⅞" squares.

Note: You could use Triangle Paper or Thangles to make HST blocks. Follow the instructions included with these products. You will have enough fabric to choose your favorite method.

Below are listed the HST fabric combinations, and how many HST of each combination needed:

R&B: 24	R&A: 36
S&A: 40	B&D: 32
S&P: 32	T&D: 16
P&T: 32	P&A: 4
P&R: 4	

Step 2

After completing the HST, cut squares 3½" x 3 ½"
from:　R: 12
　　　　S: 16
Cut 4 P squares 6½" x 6½".

Step 3

The quilt will be constructed in quarters. Each quarter is an 8 block by 8 block unit. Follow the diagram for block placement.

Step 4

Sew the four quadrants together into one unit to create a star showing in the center.

Step 5

Attach the first border.

Use: 4 R rectangles 3½" x 9½"
　　 4 R & A HST
　　 2 A strips 3½" x 24½"
Sew them together into 2 rows. Press seams open.

Sew these 2 strips to the top and bottom of the completed top, pinning to match the HST seams to those on the quilt top. Be certain that the dark triangles of the HST will be along the outside edge of the quilt. Press the seams toward these borders.

Step 6

Use: 4 R rectangles 3½" x 12½"
　　 4 R & A HST
　　 2 A strips 3½"x 24½"
Sew them together into 2 rows. Press seams open.

Sew these 2 longer strips to opposite sides of your quilt, matching seams when appropriate. Press the seams toward these borders.

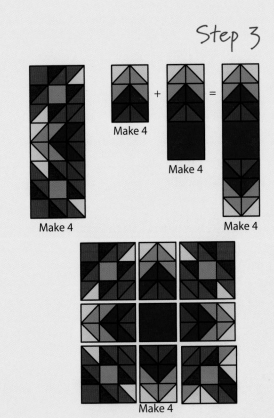

Step 3

Make 4

Make 4

Make 4　　Make 4

Make 4

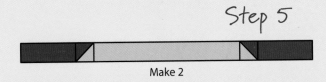

Step 5

Make 2

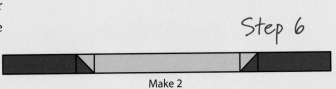

Step 6

Make 2

Step 7

Sew the remaining borders as follows:

Second border:
Sew the 6 B 1½" strips together end-to-end into one long strip. Press the seams open.

Measure down the center of the top vertically. Cut 2 borders to this length. For a perfect border fit, quarter the top and borders to create pin placement marks: fold each in half, crease, then in half again and crease. Use the crease marks as you pin raw edges together, starting at the center. If needed, ease in fullness within quarters.

Sew a border down both sides of the quilt. Press the seams toward the new border. Square the corners of the growing quilt.

Measure across the center of the quilt horizontally. Cut 2 borders to this length. Quarter and sew the remaining border strips along the top and bottom of the quilt. Press the seams to the borders and square the quilt corners.

Outer border:
Sew the 7 P 6½" strips together end-to-end into one long strip. Create and attach this outer border in the same manner as the second border, carefully squaring all 4 corners of the quilt.

You're ready to square the top, layer it with batting and backing, baste the layers, quilt as desired, and bind and label your quilt.

Quick Orzo Pilaf

This is refreshing and fast to make, after a long day quilting in the desert Southwest!

1 cup orzo

1 cup frozen corn

1 large ripe tomato
  (or 3 Roma tomatoes) chopped

2 green onions, chopped

¼ cup sliced black olives
  (optional)

1 T olive oil

¼ cup crumbled feta cheese

Bring 1 quart of salted water to a boil and cook orzo al dente. Rinse frozen corn to thaw. Drain and place in large mixing bowl. Add chopped tomatoes, onions and olives. Drain orzo and add to bowl. Drizzle olive oil over all and toss well. Top with feta.

Note: You can add 2 tablespoons of pesto sauce for more flavor; or add 2 tablespoons of soy sauce, 1 teaspoon of sesame oil, grated ginger, and sliced mushrooms for Asian pilaf.

Hint

For more accurate quilts, it's a good idea to take the time to square-up your blocks and quilt sections before proceeding to the next step. Not only does this keep your work square, but it keeps you more focused on your own accuracy.

Color Variations

LOOKS LIKE SUMMER AJO STAR
Made by Margaret Pancake
Ajo, Arizona

JEWEL TONES AJO STAR
Made by Marge Cooper
Ajo, Arizona

Color Variation

SOUTHWEAT AJO STAR
Made by Gail McBurney
Ajo, Arizona

Cheddar Rice and Quackers

3 cups cooked rice, chilled
  (you can substitute macaroni)

3 ribs celery, chopped

2 cups broccoli, chopped

1 red pepper, chopped

2 cups sharp
  cheddar cheese, shredded

1 cup Ranch dressing

½ cup salsa

1 cup oyster crackers,
  crushed

Bunch of fresh basil or
  parsley, chopped

Mix ingredients through salsa and toss gently. Chill overnight. Sprinkle with crackers and basil or parsley before serving.

Resources

Dear Quilter,

You are welcomed and encouraged to use any sewing products you favor or already have on hand to complete any of these patterns. For those who would like suggestions or recommendations for tools to complete some of the techniques more easily, I have listed the ones I used in this book's projects and recommend in my shop:

Thangles™ Triangle Paper (3" finished size)

Quiltime Half-Square and Quarter-Square Triangle Paper (3" finished)

Lazy Girl Flying Geese x 4 Ruler

Creative Grids® ⅞" Ruler

Creative Grids 8½" x 24½" Ruler

Assorted Creative Grids Rulers and sizes.

Creative Grids are designed by quilters, for quilters and are proudly made in the USA. They have fine lines, white and black, and embedded gripper-dots to prevent slipping. Visit www.creativegridsusa.com to view available sizes and watch demo-videos.

I use these items because of consistent quality, ease of use, and repeatedly successful results. These products can usually be found in your local quilt shop, or you may order them on-line from www.creationssewclever.com.

Wishing you many, happy Creations SewClever!
In Stitches,

Rita

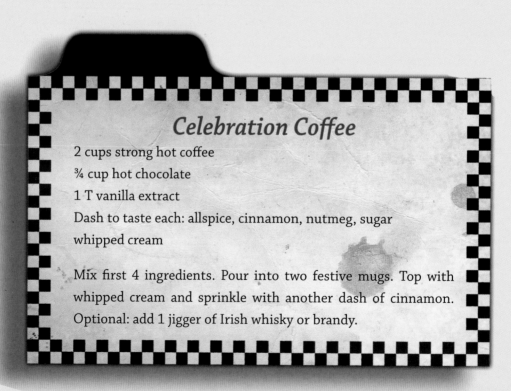

Celebration Coffee

2 cups strong hot coffee

¾ cup hot chocolate

1 T vanilla extract

Dash to taste each: allspice, cinnamon, nutmeg, sugar

whipped cream

Mix first 4 ingredients. Pour into two festive mugs. Top with whipped cream and sprinkle with another dash of cinnamon. Optional: add 1 jigger of Irish whisky or brandy.

Meet Rita Fishel

Rita Fishel is a nationally known author, speaker, and teacher. She is Goddess and Queen Mother of Creations SewClever in Chillicothe, Ohio, and national Demo-Goddess, designer, and consultant for Creative Grids USA.

A native of northeastern Ohio with a B.A. in clothing and textiles/business from the University of Akron, Rita purchased a small clothing and fabric business in 1992 and hasn't looked back.

Now located in a beautiful 1800s Georgian home, Creations SewClever is a full-line quilt shop with 3 longarm quilting machines, a friendly staff of 16 quilters, and an amusing resident ghost. When she's not there, Rita is on the road in the Stitch Mobile, sharing her passion for all-things-quilt with guilds and groups nationwide.

Stop by the shop when you find yourself in southern Ohio. The gang is dying to show you around. You'll be offered a fresh cup of coffee and continuing tales of Rita's adventures—and misadventures—in the Stitch Mobile. Visit Creations SewClever online at www.creationssewclever.com.

other AQS books

This is only a small selection of the books available from the American Quilter's Society. AQS books are known worldwide for timely topics, clear writing, beautiful color photos, and accurate illustrations and patterns. The following books are available from your local bookseller, quilt shop, or public library.

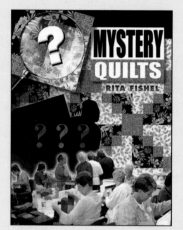

#7079 $22.95

#8027 $26.95

#8355 $24.95

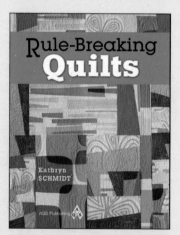

#8150 $24.95

#8346 $26.95

#8242 $22.95

#8149 $26.95

#8236 $24.95

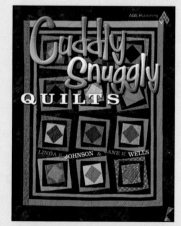

#8239 $26.95

LOOK for these books nationally.

CALL or **VISIT** our website at

1-800-626-5420

WWW.AMERICANQUILTER.COM